CONGRESS AND COUNTERSUBVERSION
IN THE 20TH CENTURY

Congress and Countersubversion in the 20th Century

Aspects and Legacies

David M. Durant

PUBLISHED BY EAST CAROLINA UNIVERSITY ACADEMIC LIBRARY SERVICES

Library of Congress Cataloging-in-Publication Data
Names: Durant, David M., author.
Title: Congress and countersubversion in the
20th century : aspects and legacies / David M. Durant.
Other titles: Congress and countersubversion in the twentieth century
Description: [Greenville, North Carolina] : East Carolina University
Academic Library Services, [2023] | Includes bibliographical references.
Identifiers: LCCN 2023017172 | ISBN 9781469677637 (paperback) |
ISBN 9781469677644 (open access ebook)
Subjects: LCSH: United States. Congress. House. Committee on
Un-American Activities. | Subversive activities—United States—History—
20th century. | Anti-communist movements—United States—History—20th
century. | Political persecution—United States—History—20th century. |
Governmental investigations—United States—History—20th century. |
Cold War. | United States—Politics and government—1901-1953. |
United States—Politics and government—1945-1989.
Classification: LCC E743.5 .D85 2023 | DDC 322.4/20973—dc23/eng/20230428
LC record available at https://lccn.loc.gov/2023017172

Suggested citation: Durant, David M.
Congress and Countersubversion in the 20th Century:
Aspects and Legacies.

DOI: https://doi.org/10.5149/9781469677644_Durant

ISBN 978-1-4696-7763-7 (paperback)
ISBN 978-1-4696-7764-4 (open access ebook)

Published by East Carolina University Academic Library Services

Distributed by the University of North Carolina Press
www.uncpress.org

TABLE OF CONTENTS

ACKNOWLEDGMENTS

Above all others, I wish to thank Jan Lewis, Director of Academic Library Services (ALS), for encouraging me to pursue this volume, and for being willing to publish it through ALS. In addition, Jan also allowed and enabled me to create and publish a blog in support of our Cold War & Internal Security Collection, whose posts make up the core of this work. Also, I must thank all of my librarian colleagues, a group far too large to mention, at ECU and elsewhere, for both supporting my research into the topics explored in this collection, and also providing me with venues in which to present on these topics and thus further develop these ideas. Special acknowledgment should be made of my immediate supervisor, Professor Jeanne Hoover, and ALS Assistant Director for Collections and Scholarly Communication, Professor Joseph Thomas, for their support of my efforts. Thanks also to the team at UNC Press's Office of Scholarly Publishing Services: John McLeod, Sam Dalzell and their staff for all of their time, patience, and assistance. Per the usual disclaimer, responsibility for any errors is entirely mine.

Finally, I wish to dedicate this work to my late parents, Charles B. and Joan L. Durant, in loving gratitude for all they did for me. They are truly the source of whatever positive characteristics I possess. In particular, by investing in a set of World Book encyclopedias, and allowing me to spend my pre K-12 afternoons reading them, they laid the groundwork for whatever intellectual achievements I have been blessed to have accomplished.

About This Volume

The core of this book consists of essays originally posted on the blog devoted to the Cold War and Internal Security (CWIS) Collection, belonging to Academic Library Services, East Carolina University. Created in 2013, the CWIS Collection includes over 2,200 volumes of congressional hearings, committee prints, committee reports, and other publications, from the House Un-American Activities Committee (HUAC), its successor the

House Committee on Internal Security (HCIS), the Senate's Permanent Subcommittee on Investigations (SPSI), the Senate Internal Security Subcommittee (SISS), and other congressional and executive bodies, all covering the years 1918–1977. The contents of the collection cover congressional investigations of organizations deemed "subversive" or "un-American", primarily the Communist Party USA (CPUSA) and its allies. Other subjects of investigation include the New Left, the Ku Klux Klan, the Black Panthers, 1930s and 40s pro-Nazi organizations, and even the World War II internment of Japanese-Americans. These items serve as valuable primary sources on topics such as American political culture during the Depression, World War II and the Cold War; the history of American Communism and the other investigated movements; the fate of civil liberties during a period of perceived external threat; foreign espionage and influence operations; and the evolution of attitudes toward political movements deemed extreme or "un-American".

The CWIS Collection is part of the Association of Southeast Regional Libraries' Collaborative Federal Depository Program, and of the US Government Publishing Office's Preservation Steward program.

In creating the CWIS Blog and its contents, I sought a means to promote the collection, not just by increasing awareness of its existence, but also by exploring the history contained within these usually drab-looking volumes. In particular, I wished to show the relevance of the CWIS Collection by illustrating its importance as a set of primary source materials on topics that continue to be addressed in the present. One thing I did not anticipate in 2013 was precisely just how relevant many of these subjects would prove to be over the ensuing decade.

I have made 53 posts on the CWIS Blog since April 2013. Of these, about 30 have been incorporated in this volume in some fashion. In a number of cases, posts have been combined to avoid redundancy, or otherwise revised or edited. The end result is a collection of 24 brief essays, each in some way relevant to the content of, or historical themes addressed by the CWIS Collection. These essays have been organized into five chronological/topical sections. There is also an introductory essay that explores the broader history behind this collection and helps put this material into context. Each brief essay contains its own list of sources. Many sources will be found listed in multiple essays. While this makes for some redundancy, it also allows each entry to stand alone if needed.

The first section, "From Brewing to Brown Scare: 1917–1945," covers the birth of 20th Century congressional countersubversive investigations in the

First World War and aftermath of the Bolshevik Revolution. It then addresses the rise of left countersubversion and the origins of the House Un-American Activities Committee, then finally the tragic injustice that was the internment of Japanese-Americans in World War Two.

Part two, "McCarthyism and Red Scare: 1946–1959," is the largest of the five sections, covering the time period that most people think of when it comes to congressional countersubversive investigations. A mix of congressional and private sector actors ensured that a process that could have been confined to investigations of Soviet/CPUSA espionage became an all-out search for communists at every level of American society, with consequences to civil liberties far in excess of any possible national security benefit.

The third section is the shortest, covering the period from 1960 to 1977, the year that the last congressional countersubversive committee, the Senate Internal Security Subcommittee, was shuttered. This period saw the rise of the New Left, the Civil Rights Revolution, Vietnam, Watergate, the end of the Cold War consensus, and a general loss of trust in authority that spelled the demise of Congress's ability to investigate domestic subversion.

Part four concerns the broader Cold War espionage and political/information struggle. As the source lists from this section show, committees such as HUAC devoted much of their time to investigating Soviet intelligence, propaganda activities, and even human rights violations. In addition, the topics featured in this section contain great relevance to the present. Communist allegations regarding Korean War biological weapons and the origins of AIDS helped set the stage for current disinformation regarding COVID and COVID vaccines. The Katyn Forest Massacre has come to epitomize in some ways the struggle between Russia and her western neighbors over the history of the Second World War, a phenomenon that is very much tied to the current war in Ukraine.

These essays also offer a useful segue to part five, which discusses post-1977 topics that reflect the continued salience of many of the historical themes from the era of congressional countersubversion. As discussed below, subversion and countersubversion remain sadly relevant to the present.

By its very nature, this work is not intended as a comprehensive history of its subject. Rather, it is designed to serve as an introduction, and to hopefully inspire further exploration of these topics. Thus, this volume can serve as a gateway for additional research, involving both secondary works and the published primary sources produced by the various federal investigative bodies.

Introductory Essay: Congress and Countersubversion
in the Twentieth Century

It is beyond the scope of this essay to offer anything like a comprehensive history of countersubversion in American history. While the countersubversive impulse dates back to the earliest days of the American Republic, it took the 20th Century emergence of the congressional committee investigation in its broad, sweeping form that enabled the mix of federal, state/local, and civil society activism that defined American countersubversion from World War One through the 1970s.

The Origins of American Countersubversion

Fear of subversive and threatening conspiracies can be found in the very beginnings of the United States. In fact, the first countersubversive effort in American history came in 1798, with the passage of the Alien and Sedition Laws by a Federalist-controlled Congress, motivated by fear that their Democratic-Republican foes planned to stage a French Jacobin-style revolution.

Fear of subversive conspiracies continued into the 19th Century. Before the Civil War, for example, many in the North feared that Southern elites constituted a "slave power" conspiracy, that would subvert the liberties of Northern whites. Southerners obsessed over Northern abolitionist and anti-slavery sentiment, in turn feared a conspiracy to undermine their "peculiar institution."

As the culture of countersubversion developed over the course of the 19th Century, so did the idea of Americanism. The notion of Americanism emerged in the Jacksonian Era. Historian David Brion Davis describes the rise of Americanism as representing a combination of belief in the ideas of progress and individualism with a commitment to tradition as represented by the legacy of the Founding Fathers. In his words:

> With only a loose and often ephemeral attachment to places and institutions, many Americans felt a compelling need to articulate their loyalties, to prove their faith, and to demonstrate their allegiance to certain ideals and institutions. By doing so, they acquired a sense of self-identity and personal direction in an otherwise rootless and shifting environment. (Davis, "Some Themes of Countersubversion," 65)

There were three groups that were increasingly seen as alien threats to this emerging American "sense of self-identity and personal direction:"

Freemasons, Catholics, and Mormons. As they looked at these three disparate communities, "nativists discerned a group of unscrupulous leaders plotting to subvert the American social order. Though rank-and-file members were not individually evil, they were blinded and corrupted by a persuasive ideology that justified treason and gross immorality in the interest of the subversive group.... these dupes.... labored unknowingly to abolish free society, to enslave their fellow men, and to overthrow divine principles of law and justice." (Davis, "Some Themes of Countersubversion," 64)

Here, in this description, one sees the template that would be applied throughout the 20th Century to groups deemed un-American or subversive.

This mid-1800s countersubversive wave would even lead to the first legislative countersubversive investigation in American history. In February 1855, the Massachusetts state legislature, overwhelmingly controlled by the anti-Catholic "Know-Nothings," formed a joint committee to investigate Catholic schools, convents, and other institutions, in order to find evidence of Papal conspiracies and the other gross iniquities that Know-Nothings were convinced must be taking place in these locations. The committee enjoyed a short and ignominious life.

Notions of Americanism and fears of subversion would linger throughout the rest of the 19th Century. They would reemerge stronger than ever when America entered the First World War in 1917. Now simple Americanism wasn't enough. "One Hundred Percent Americanism" was required. Scholar Stanley Cohen has offered a useful if controversial description of what this entailed:

> Its objective was to end the apparent erosion of American values and the disintegration of American culture. By reaffirming those beliefs, customs, symbols, and traditions felt to be the foundation of our way of life, by enforcing conformity among the population, and by purging the nation of dangerous foreigners, the one hundred percenters expected to heal societal divisions and to tighten defenses against cultural change. (Cohen, "The American Red Scare," 154)

Bringing Congress Into the Picture

One feature of 19th Century countersubversion was that it occurred mainly at state and local level. There was no attempt by Congress to conduct a countersubversive investigation until 1871–72, when a joint House-Senate committee examined the terrorist activities of the Ku Klux Klan during Reconstruction.

This was not an accident. As Telford Taylor has noted, congressional committee investigations during the first century of the American republic focused
almost exclusively on the activities of the executive branch of the federal government. It was not until the 1880s that Congress began to take upon itself
the power to look into broader societal conditions. The Progressive Era, with
its combination of disruptive social phenomena such as immigration and in-
dustrialization, along with the growing belief in a more expansive role for
the federal government, soon led to a drastic rise in the quantity and scope
of congressional committee investigations. According to the ProQuest Congressional database, the transcripts of 830 congressional hearings were published between 1871–1900, with another 296 hearings going unpublished.
From 1901–1915, 4,205 hearings were published, with another 194 unpublished. This five-fold increase in the number of published hearing transcripts
is indicative of the massive growth of congressional investigations in the early
20th Century.

Fueling this increase was a growing belief that Congress's investigative
power was virtually unlimited in scope. As future Supreme Court Justice Fe-
lix Frankfurter wrote in 1924: "no limitations should be imposed by congressional legislation or standing rules. The power of investigation should be left
untrammeled." (Quoted in Taylor, *Grand Inquest*, 61)

It was the combination of these three factors: a culture of countersubversion targeting those deemed "un-American;" the concept of Americanism
as an ideal that must be protected from hostile and alien influences; and the
expansion of Congress's willingness to investigate broader social phenomena,
ultimately including potential subversion, that made the 20th Century's brand
of countersubversion possible.

Overall Themes

As you read through the entries in this volume, a number of connecting themes will emerge. Here are four main principles to keep in mind when stud-
ying the history of 20th Century countersubversion:

1. Generally speaking, countersubversive panics arose in response to
    actual threats, not imagined ones. Imperial Germany did engage in
    an extensive campaign of sabotage and subversion in the United
    States between 1914–1917. There was a genuine upsurge in left-wing

radicalism in 1918–19, much of it inspired by the example of the Bolshevik Revolution. Attorney General A. Mitchell Palmer, the figure most closely associated with the first "Red Scare," actually had a bomb detonated on the front porch of his home. There were any number of radical right movements that emerged in the 1930s, some openly inspired by Nazi Germany and Fascist Italy. The Communist Party USA was slavishly loyal to the USSR, and did in fact infiltrate the American government to carry out espionage, in cooperation with Soviet intelligence services. The most important thing about the countersubversive impulse was not that it fabricated nonexistent threats, but rather that it often inspired a thoroughly exaggerated view of these threats, as well as completely disproportionate and even counter-productive responses to them. What were discrete phenomena were treated by countersubversives as simply the most radical edge of broader American trends and movements they despised. Most infamously, this can be seen in the segregationist efforts to treat the civil rights movement as a communist front.

2. Contrary to much popular belief, countersubversion was not, and is not, the exclusive province of the right. It was after all a liberal Jewish Democrat from New York City who was the driving force behind the establishment of the House Un-American Activities Committee in the 1930s. The Roosevelt Administration and New Dealers in Congress were perfectly willing to use the power of the federal government to curb the growth of right-wing radicalism as part of what has been called the "Brown Scare."

Many radical right organizations and individuals who embraced the countersubversive ethos found themselves the target of Left Countersubversion during the Brown Scare. Elizabeth Dilling, author of the infamous 1934 guilt-by-association work *The Red Network*, was put on trial for pro-Axis sedition during World War Two, along with nearly 30 other defendants. As loathsome as Dilling and many of the other defendants were, the great sedition trial of 1944 (United States v. McWilliams) is generally considered a travesty of justice.

By the same token, the CPUSA during the Popular Front period of the late 1930s touted itself as representing "Twentieth Century Americanism." While of course a major victim of countersubversive political persecution, especially from 1947–1960, the party had no objections when the federal government used countersubversive methods against its adversaries. Communists vehemently denounced the use of the Smith Act of 1940 to prosecute CPUSA leaders, yet supported the same Smith Act when it was used against their Trotskyite foes. They also supported the various federal efforts directed against the radical right, such as the 1944 sedition trial.

In some ways the history of 20th Century American countersubversion is the history of rival forms of countersubversion, each rooted in a different sense of what it meant to be American, and thus what was "Un-American."

3. The countersubversive impulse is not synonymous with anti-communism, nor, for that matter, with anti-fascism. While there were both anti-communist and anti-fascist forms of countersubversion, neither fully embodied the diversity of belief and motivation in either intellectual trend. As Richard Gid Powers and others have noted, there were many versions of anti-communism. In addition to the radical-right/hard conservative notion that communism was merely the cutting edge of a dangerous left determined to overthrow decent American society, other forms of anti-communism were rooted in concrete aspects of Soviet and CPUSA behavior. Catholic anti-communism for example, was a response to Soviet religious repression. Liberal anti-communism was a reaction to Soviet totalitarian oppression and external aggrandizement. There was even a social democratic anti-communism, rooted in the experience of being on the receiving end of the CPUSA's often vicious and sectarian efforts to control labor unions, political groups, and other organizations.

In the same manner, there were likewise a number of strains of anti-fascism. Communists and their allies regarded fascism as simply the final stage of monopoly capitalism, and thus were extremely flexible regarding what and whom they considered "fascist." Jewish advocacy organizations were justifiably alarmed by Nazi anti-Semitism, which was also an all too common trait among the American radical right of the 1930s. New Deal liberals feared that domestic fascism threatened our democratic system. While these various versions of anti-communism and anti-fascism overlapped with countersubversion to some degree, most cannot be defined by it.

4. The final theme, which will be explicitly addressed in Part Five, is the alarming extent to which many of the themes surrounding subversion and countersubversion strongly echo in our present political environment. The term "active measures" was merely a footnote to Cold War history, until Russia's effort to influence the 2016 US election on behalf of Donald Trump gave the concept a disturbing new relevance. Similarly, our present polarization evokes parallels with the bitter divisions and growing extremism of American politics in the 1930s. In particular, the rise of White nationalist acts of terror, and the January 6th putsch attempt at the Capital, raise some of the same fears of the radical right that produced the Brown Scare. The existence of such legitimate threats, and the need to avoid overreacting to them, show that while the era of congressional countersubversion ended in the 1970s, the countersubversive legacy remains as timely and relevant as ever.

Sources

Cohen, Stanley. "The American Red Scare of 1919–1920." in *Conspiracy: The Fear of Subversion in American History*. ed. Richard O. Curry and Thomas M. Brown. New York: Holt, Rinehart and Winston, Inc, 1972, 144–157.

Davis, David Brion. "Some Themes of Countersubversion: An Analysis of Anti-Masonic, Anti-Catholic, and Anti-Mormon Literature." in *Conspiracy: The Fear of Subversion in American History*. ed. Richard O. Curry and Thomas M. Brown. New York: Holt, Rinehart and Winston, Inc, 1972, 61–77.

Morgan, Ted. *Reds: McCarthyism in Twentieth-Century America*. New York: Random House, 2003.

Powers, Richard Gid. *Not Without Honor: The History of American Anticommunism*. New York: Free Press, 1995.

Ribuffo, Leo P. *The Old Christian Right: The Protestant Far Right from the Great Depression to the Cold War*. Philadelphia: Temple University Press, 1983.

Taylor, Telford. *Grand Inquest: The Story of Congressional Investigation*. New York: Simon and Schuster, 1955.

Trelease, Allen W. *White Terror: The Ku Klux Klan Conspiracy and Southern Reconstruction*. New York: Harper & Row, 1971.

PART ONE

From Brewing to Brown Scare

1917–1945

Beer, Subversion, and Bolsheviks

World War I and the First Investigative Committee

Senator Lee Slater Overman (D-NC), 1854–1930, chairman of the Senate Judiciary Subcommittee, pictured here circa 1910. Overman, a native of Salisbury, served in the Senate from 1903 till his death. Library of Congress Prints & Photographs Division: https://www.loc.gov/item/2005683904/.

WHEN AMERICA ENTERED THE FIRST WORLD WAR in April 1917, the country witnessed a major upsurge of nationalistic sentiment, encouraged and often instigated by the federal government. Through a combination of governmental bodies such as the Committee on Public Information (CPI), dubbed America's "first ministry of information," and private organizations such as the American Protective League (APL), popular intolerance of anti-war sentiment, and fear of pro-German and radical subversion, reached a fever pitch.

It is thus unsurprising that World War One spawned what historian Alex Goodall has called "the first countersubversive investigative committee in American history." While Goodall's contention ignores the existence of several 19th Century state and federal legislative committees with countersubversive mandates, he is right to acknowledge the historic importance of this particular body. (Goodall, *Loyalty and Liberty*, 45) A subcommittee of the Senate Judiciary Committee, chaired by North Carolina's first popularly-elected senator, and briefly immortalized in the 1981 Academy Award winning film *Reds*, the colorfully named Subcommittee to Investigate Brewing and Liquor Interests and German and Bolshevik Propaganda set the stage for all the countersubversive investigations to come.

The Overman Committee

Fear of German-sponsored subversion was widespread upon the USA's entry into World War One. While such worries were certainly stoked by the CPI, the popular press, and groups such as the APL, it is important to note that German efforts at espionage, sabotage, and subversion were more than merely the figments of overheated imaginations. In the words of historian Francis MacDonnell:

> During the period from 1914–17, the Central Powers mounted repeated acts of intrigue against America. The German and Austrian embassies supervised this clandestine warfare. It included attempts to forge passports, blow up bridges, incite labor unrest, disrupt munitions production, and plant incendiary devices aboard merchant ships. (MacDonnell, *Insidious Foes*, 11–12)

A particular concern was the brewing industry, dominated as it was by individuals of German descent. In this, wartime fears merged with prohibitionist and anti-immigrant sentiment. A. Mitchell Palmer, the Attorney General, openly denounced the brewing industry for being both a source of funding for pro-German subversion as well as inducing moral corruption. In response to Palmer's accusations, the Senate, in September 1918, passed Resolution 307, which created a subcommittee of the Senate Judiciary Committee tasked with investigating "Brewing and Liquor Interests and German Propaganda."

The subcommittee consisted of five members. Chairing the group was North Carolina's Lee Overman. A senator since 1903, Overman made history in 1914 when, in the wake of the passage of the 17th Amendment to the constitution in 1913, he became North Carolina's first popularly elected senator. Overman was a loyal supporter of President Woodrow Wilson, and strongly opposed to immigration.

The new subcommittee held its first hearing on September 27, 1918, and continued its investigation into early 1919. By the end, the committee had branched out beyond the brewing industry into a broader look at German espionage and subversion. The Overman committee documented a campaign by the Imperial German government to pursue "extensive and far-reaching acts of violence," directed at the American munitions industry, as well as a widespread effort to fund and disseminate pro-Central Powers propaganda. (*Brewing and Liquor Interests*, v.1, XIII)

The Overman committee's work also reflected not only wartime fears, but prevailing concerns about the importance of preserving "Americanism," and the dangers allegedly posed by large populations of unassimilated immigrants. Its report stated that "a large number" of foreign language publications were "unpatriotic and disloyal to the United States, its principles and institutions." English-language newspapers that opposed the war were denounced by the committee as encouraging "Germany and German sympathizers." (*Brewing and Liquor Interests*, v.1, XXVII)

In terms of the brewing industry, the Overman committee found that they sought to fund, influence, and gain control over numerous politicians, news outlets, and civic organizations. While not directly charged by the subcommittee with aiding the German war effort, the negative publicity the hearings generated for the brewing industry coincided with the ratification of the Eighteenth Amendment (Prohibition) in January 1919. In the words of Goodall, "the publicity surrounding Overman's hearings undoubtedly contributed to the final push for Prohibition." (Goodall, *Loyalty and Liberty*, 28)

Turning Attention to Bolshevism

In February 1919, with the defeat of Imperial Germany, and growing fears of radicalism sparked by the Bolshevik Revolution in Russia, the Senate passed Resolution 436, expanding the mandate of the Overman subcommittee to include the study of Bolshevik-related subversion.

The committee began its hearings into Bolshevism on February 11, 1919. In so doing it became the first congressional committee investigation into communism. In hearings running until March 10, 1919, the Overman committee heard testimony from roughly 25 witnesses. Ironically, in light of the committee's countersubversive mandate, the bulk of its investigation focused on conditions in Russia and the nature of the Bolshevik regime.

Most witnesses were anti-Bolshevik, but it was the handful of pro-Bolshevik witnesses who provided some of the most memorable testimony. Most notably, on February 20–21, the radical journalist John Reed, and his wife, Louise Bryant, appeared before the Overman committee. The confrontation between the conservative southerner Overman and the radical feminist Bryant was particularly heated at times. Her testimony was marked, as Goodall puts it, by a "deeply gendered hostility" that "produced an almost total impasse between witness and senators." (Goodall, *Loyalty and Liberty*, 52) This confrontation was briefly portrayed in the 1981 Warren Beatty film *Reds*, with Diane Keaton playing the role of Louise Bryant, and dialogue taken directly from the official transcript.

In its final report, published in July 1919, the Overman committee correctly noted that "only a portion of the so-called radical revolutionary groups and organizations accept in its entirety the doctrine of the Bolsheviki." The committee nonetheless insisted that domestic radicalism was still a threat:

> The radical revolutionary elements in this country and the Bolshevik government of Russia have, therefore, found a common cause in support of which they can unite their forces. They are both fanning the flame of discontent and endeavoring to incite revolution. (*Brewing and Liquor Interests*, v.1, XLII)

Conclusion

As the first congressional countersubversive committee of the 20th Century, the Overman committee established the precedent that ultimately led to HUAC, the Senate Internal Security Subcommittee, and the activities of Senator Joseph McCarthy. It also reflected the trend among countersubversives to tie the threat of foreign or domestic radical subversion to broader social phenomena that they found disturbing, such as fear of further immigration, and worries over unassimilated immigrants. The Overman committee, for example, insisted on "the necessity of Americanizing the residents of this country." (*Brewing and Liquor Interests*, v.1, XLVII)

The notion of "Americanism" represented by the Overman committee and its successors remained a potent force in American society until the cultural revolution of the 1960s. When it found itself marginalized in the wake of that revolution, the countersubversive committees it spawned quickly vanished.

Primary Source

Brewing and Liquor Interests and German and Bolshevik Propaganda: Report and Hearings of the Subcommittee on the Judiciary, United States Senate, Submitted Pursuant to S. Res. 307 and 439, Sixty-Fifth Congress, Relating to Charges Made Against the United States Brewers' Association and Allied Interests. 3 vols. Washington, D.C.: Government Printing Office, 1919.

Additional Sources

Daly, Christopher B. "How Woodrow Wilson's Propaganda Machine Changed American Journalism." Smithsonian.com, April 28, 2017. https://www .smithsonianmag.com/history/how-woodrow-wilsons-propaganda-machine -changed-american-journalism-180963082/.

Eagles, Brenda Marks. "Overman, Lee Slater." *Dictionary of North Carolina Biography*. Chapel Hill: University of North Carolina Press, 1991. https://www.ncpedia.org/biography/overman-lee-slater.

Goodall, Alex. *Loyalty and Liberty: American Countersubversion from World War I to the McCarthy Era*. Urbana: University of Illinois Press, 2013.

Inman, Michael. "Spies Among Us: World War I and The American Protective League." *New York Public Library* (blog), October 14, 2014. https://www.nypl .org/blog/2014/10/07/spies-among-us-wwi-apl.

MacDonnell, Francis. *Insidious Foes: The Axis Fifth Column and the American Home Front*. New York: Oxford University Press, 1995.

Morgan, Ted. *Reds: McCarthyism in Twentieth-Century America*. New York: Random House, 2003.

2

The Left Embraces Countersubversion

The 1930s Brown Scare and the Growth of Countersubversion

John Metcalfe, first witness to appear before the House Special Committee on Un-American Activities, discussed his experience infiltrating the German-American Bund, August 12, 1938. Source: Harris & Ewing Collection, Library of Congress Prints and Photographs Division: https://www.loc.gov/resource/hec.24931/

THE RISE OF ADOLF HITLER'S NAZI PARTY to power in Germany in 1933 inspired the creation of a number of radical right-wing movements here in the United States. The most infamous of these groups, was the Friends of New Germany, who in 1936 would rename themselves the German-American Bund and openly pattern themselves on and embrace German Nazism. Other groups included William Dudley Pelley's Silver Legion of America (the "Silver Shirts"), Father Charles Coughlin's Christian Front, and the Black Legion. The latter group was involved in several murders in the industrial Midwest, and became so infamous that they were the subject of a 1936 Warner Brothers film starring Humphrey Bogart.

This growth in domestic fascism and right-wing radicalism soon produced what historian Leo Ribuffo has called the "Brown Scare": an often exaggerated fear of the threat posed by the radical right, in response to the alarming rise of the Third Reich in Europe and the frequently repellent activities of its supporters in the U.S.

Numerous individuals and organizations warned of the dangers believed to be posed by domestic fascism, both in news media and popular culture. In addition to films like *Black Legion*, Sinclair Lewis's ironically titled 1935 novel *It Can't Happen Here* warned of a fascist takeover of America. A number of civil society organizations also led the charge against the emerging radical right. Groups such as the Friends of Democracy, Non-Sectarian Anti-Nazi League, and Mobilization for Democracy, exposed real and alleged fascist activities and mobilized public opinion against the newly-perceived threat.

The Roosevelt Administration and its allies in Congress likewise embraced the politics of the Brown Scare. Among other consequences, it would lead a New Deal Democrat, Rep. Samuel Dickstein (D-NY), to play a crucial role in creating what would become the House Un-American Activities Committee. (See next entry) FDR himself was committed to using the power of the federal government to root out domestic fascism, regardless of civil liberties concerns. It was Roosevelt who empowered J. Edgar Hoover and the FBI to engage in domestic political surveillance, starting in 1934.

As the perceived threat posed by foreign and domestic fascism grew, the Brown Scare only intensified. At home, events such as the 1938 discovery of a Nazi spy ring in New York City, and the German-American Bund's infamous February 1939 rally at Madison Square Garden increased pressure to act against the radical right. Abroad, the continued successes of Nazi Germany and Fascist Italy contributed to the growing concerns. One especially infamous quote uttered in the fall of 1936, during the Spanish Civil War, came to encapsulate this environment. In an offhand comment, Spanish Nationalist General Emilio Mola referred to a nationalist "fifth column" that would capture the city of Madrid from within. The phrase "fifth column" soon went "viral," to borrow a contemporary term, spreading rapidly around the world. In the American context, it came to embody the fear that the Bund, Silver Shirts, and other domestic fascists could be used by the Third Reich to weaken and subvert the US from within.

FDR openly adopted the idea of the "fifth column" to justify acting against domestic fascist groups. On May 26, 1940, in the midst of Germany's relatively quick victories in western Europe, Roosevelt warned in a radio address about "the Trojan Horse. The Fifth Column that betrays a nation unprepared for treachery." He went on to elaborate by stating that this internal enemy would seek "to create confusion of counsel, public indecision, political paralysis and, eventually, a state of panic…. The unity of the State can be sapped so that its strength is destroyed." (U.S. Holocaust Memorial Museum, 'Roosevelt's Address on the "Fifth Column"')

Powered by such fears, the Brown Scare soon culminated in a campaign of legal persecution at federal, state, and local level. Both the head of the Bund, Fritz Kuhn, and the Silver Shirts, William Dudley Pelley, were arrested and tried. Kuhn was convicted in New York in 1939 for embezzling Bund funds, sent to prison, and eventually deported. Pelley was convicted by the federal government in 1942 on charges of sedition. He then became one of 30 defendants charged in the 1944 mass sedition case, United States v. McWilliams. This case would end in a mistrial after the death of the judge. This trial marked the end of the Brown Scare. The defeat of the Axis both discredited fascism and greatly reduced its salience as a domestic threat. In addition, the onset of the Cold War and the rise of the Second Red Scare would soon once again give right-wing countersubversion the upper hand.

As with the Red Scare of 1919–1920, the Brown Scare of 1933–1944 was rooted in a real threat, yet greatly exaggerated both the extent and scale of that threat. In the words of historian Alex Goodall:

> The groups and individuals on the radical Right that might be reasonably described as fascist or cryptofascist…. added up to a tiny fraction of the population: no more than a few hundred thousand people in a nation of 130 million…. Right-wing extremists could cause trouble in their localities, but were largely impotent on the national stage. Noxious

as they were, they never presented a meaningful threat to American institutions or spoke for more than a tiny minority of American citizens. (Goodall, *Loyalty and Liberty*, 194.)

The major legacy of the Brown Scare was the manner in which it helped prepare the way for future countersubversive measures that gravely threatened civil liberties. The "fifth column" panic was one of a number of factors that led to the internment of Japanese-Americans in 1942. The Brown Scare's mix of congressional investigation, executive branch law enforcement/surveillance activities, and civic activism provided a template for McCarthyism and the Second Red Scare. As historian John Earl Haynes described it:

> Much of the popular image of American communism that appeared after 1945 was based on attitudes developed in the 1930s and early 1940s toward fascism.... And the techniques developed to fight American fascism and American fifth-column activity in the 1930s were the same as those used against American Communists in the late 1940s and 1950s. (Haynes, *Red Scare or Red Menace*, 19)

Finally, the willingness of some to label any opponent of the New Deal, or of American entry into World War II as fascist or pro-Nazi left many right-wing countersubversives with a keen desire to return the favor. They would eagerly seize on the opportunity to do so during the McCarthy Era.

Sources

Goodall, Alex. *Loyalty and Liberty: American Countersubversion from World War I to the McCarthy Era*. Urbana: University of Illinois Press, 2013.

Haynes, John Earl. *Red Scare or Red Menace? American Communism and Anticommunism in the Cold War Era*. Chicago: Ivan R. Dee, 1996.

Ribuffo, Leo P. *The Old Christian Right: The Protestant Far Right from the Great Depression to the Cold War*. Philadelphia: Temple University Press, 1983.

Smith, Geoffrey S. *To Save a Nation; American Countersubversives, the New Deal, and the Coming of World War II*. New York: Basic Books, 1973.

United States Holocaust Memorial Museum. 'Roosevelt's Address on the "Fifth Column".' Propaganda and the American Public. https://perspectives.ushmm .org/item/roosevelts-address-on-the-fifth-column.

3

"Father of the Committee"

Rep. Samuel Dickstein and the Origins of HUAC

Rep. Samuel Dickstein (D-NY), second from right, March 1937. Source: Harris & Ewing Collection, Library of Congress Prints and Photographs Division: http://www.loc.gov/pictures/item/hec2009009088/

WHEN EXAMINING THE HISTORY of the House Un-American Activities Committee, one soon discovers an amazing irony. While HUAC spent over three decades developing a reputation as a right-wing scourge of communists real or alleged, the congressman who first conceived the idea of a committee to investigate "un-American activities" was a New Deal liberal worried about the threat of subversion posed by domestic Nazis and fascists. Even more incredibly, that same congressman, dubbed by HUAC scholar Walter Goodman as the "Father of the Committee", actually spent several years as a paid agent of the Soviet Union.

Born in 1885, Rep. Samuel Dickstein (D-NY) emigrated to the U.S. as a small child and grew up in New York City. He went to law school and became involved in the Democratic Party, serving in various state offices before winning election to Congress in 1922. Dickstein was alarmed by the Nazi seizure of power in Germany in 1933 and by the often well-publicized activities of Nazi sympathizers and native fascists in the United States. At his urging, on March 20, 1934 the House of Representatives passed House Resolution 198 (H. Res. 73–2), which created a special committee to investigate:

1. "The extent, character, and objects of Nazi propaganda activities" in the U.S.
2. "The diffusion within the United States of subversive propaganda that is instigated from foreign countries and attacks the principle of the form of government as guaranteed by our Constitution"
3. "All other questions in relation thereto" (To Authorize Special Committee, 4934)

The House Special Committee on Un-American Activities, widely considered the forerunner to HUAC, contained seven members. Rep. John McCormack (D-MA) served as Chair with Dickstein as Vice-Chair. The McCormick-Dickstein committee, as it was popularly known, primarily investigated the activities of far-right extremists such as the German-American Bund and the Silver Legion of America, but did also investigate the Communist Party as well.

The McCormick-Dickstein Committee published its report on February 15, 1935. This report included the following summation of the 1930s counter-subversive worldview:

"To the true and real American, communism, naziism (sic.), and fascism are all equally dangerous, equally alien and equally unacceptable to American institutions." (*Investigation*, 23)

The Special Committee on Un-American Activities disbanded after releasing its report. Dickstein, however, continued his campaign against alleged Nazi and fascist subversion. In early 1937, he called for the creation of a new committee on un-American activities, with a charge even more sweeping than that given to the 1934–35 version. In his ever more strident warnings about the threat posed by the German-American Bund and other far-right groups, Dickstein became one of the most prominent voices of what historian Leo Ribuffo has called the "Brown Scare": an exaggerated fear of the threat posed by domestic Nazis and fascists in response to the alarming rise of the Third Reich in Europe and the often repellent activities of its supporters in the U.S.

By this time, Dickstein had adopted the practice of denouncing by name individuals, businesses and organizations he suspected of Nazi or fascist sympathies in speeches on the floor of Congress. When six individuals identified by Dickstein as Bund members submitted signed affidavits denying the charge, Dickstein responded on the House floor on December 21, 1937 as follows:

> I have always protected character and reputation in respect to any name I have inserted in the RECORD, and I say to the membership of the House that if out of these hundreds of names that I have buttonholed as Fascists and Nazis, or whatever I have called them, only six filed a protest, I think I have done a pretty good job. (Dickstein, "Extension of Remarks," 2031)

Dickstein's desire to see a new Special Committee on Un-American Activities came to fruition on May 26, 1938, when the House passed House Res. 282, creating the committee that would become HUAC and continue in several incarnations until 1975. The resolution was sponsored by Rep. Martin Dies (D-TX), with Dickstein's full support and cooperation. However, Dies was appointed Chair while Dickstein was left off the committee altogether. The Dies Committee would direct the majority of its investigative focus on the CPUSA and New Deal, much to Dickstein's chagrin. As Goodman memorably phrased it, Dickstein was "relentless" in his efforts "from 1933 to 1938" to bring HUAC into being, only to find that he "had the rest of his life to regret" his efforts (Goodman, *The Committee*, 3).

The story of Samuel Dickstein and the origins of HUAC took an even more bizarre turn in 1999, when Allen Weinstein and Alexander Vassiliev released their book *The Haunted Wood*. Based on research in KGB archives, Weinstein and Vassiliev revealed that Dickstein maintained a covert relationship with the NKVD (Soviet secret police: predecessor of the KGB) from 1937–1940. Motivated primarily by financial incentives, Dickstein was given the code name "Crook" by the NKVD and was paid approximated $12,000 during this period. The Soviets severed the relationship with Dickstein in 1940, unhappy that they were not getting their money's worth. (Weinstein & Vassiliev, *The Haunted Wood*, Chapter 7)

This leaves us with the ultimate irony that the man who did more than any other to bring the House Un-American Activities Committee into being was on the payroll of Soviet intelligence while doing so.

After resigning from Congress in 1945, Dickstein became a justice of the New York State Supreme Court, serving there until his death in 1954.

Primary Sources

Investigation of Nazi and Other Propaganda, House Report No. 153, 74th Congress (74–1), Serial Set 9890. Washington, D.C.: Government Printing Office, 1935.

Investigation of Nazi Propaganda Activities and Investigation of Certain Other Propaganda Activities. Public Hearings Before the Special Committee on Un-American Activities, House of Representatives, Seventy-Third Congress, Second Session. 8 vols. Washington, D.C.: Government Printing Office, 1934–35.

Investigation of Un-American Propaganda Activities in the United States: Appendix. Special Committee on Un-American Activities, House of Representatives. 9 vols. Washington, D.C.: Government Printing Office, 1940–44.

Investigation of Un-American Propaganda Activities in the United States: Executive Hearings. Special Committee on Un-American Activities, House of Representatives. 7 vols. Washington, D.C.: Government Printing Office, 1939–43.

Investigation of Un-American Propaganda Activities in the United States: Hearings Before a Special Committee on Un-American Activities, House of Representatives. 17 vols. Washington, D.C.: Government Printing Office, 1938–44.

Samuel Dickstein (NY). "Extension of Remarks." *Congressional Record.* 75th Cong., 2nd sess., 1937. Vol. 82, pt. 2: 2031. Text from: Congressional Record Permanent Digital Collection.

To Authorize Special Committee to Investigate Nazi Propaganda Activities and Certain Other Propaganda Activities. HR 198. *Congressional Record.* 73rd

Cong., 2nd sess., 1934. Vol. 78 pt. 5: 4934. Text from: Congressional Record Permanent Digital Collection.

Additional Sources

"Dickstein, Samuel (1885–1954)." *Biographical Directory of the United States Congress*. https://bioguide.congress.gov/search/bio/D000335.

Goodman, Walter. *The Committee: The Extraordinary Career of the House Committee on Un-American Activities*. New York: Farrar, Straus, and Giroux, 1968.

Ribuffo, Leo P. *The Old Christian Right: The Protestant Far Right from the Great Depression to the Cold War*. Philadelphia: Temple University Press, 1983.

Weinstein, Allen and Alexander Vassiliev. *The Haunted Wood: Soviet Espionage in America–The Stalin Era*. New York: Random House, 1999.

4

"A Grave Injustice"

The Internment of Japanese-Americans, 1942–45

"Exclusion Order posted at First and Front Streets directing removal of persons of Japanese ancestry." Taken by Dorothea Lange, San Francisco, California, April 11, 1942. Central Photographic File of the War Relocation Authority, 1942 – 1945, National Archives: https://catalog.archives.gov/id/536017

THIS SPRING MARKS THE 75th anniversary of one of the gravest affronts to civil liberty in American history, the forcible internment of an estimated 117,000 Japanese-Americans living in the states of California, Oregon, Washington, and Arizona in the spring of 1942. A complex combination of fear and anger sparked by the Japanese attack on Pearl Harbor and subsequent victories in the Pacific, paranoid countersubversive fear of a "fifth column," and long-standing racial prejudice, all converged in the two months following Pearl Harbor to create an almost irresistible momentum in favor of the deportation of Japanese-Americans from the west coast. While the House Special Committee on Un-American Activities played no real role in bringing about internment, it did hold hearings that attempted to justify the federal government's actions.

"A Jap's a Jap": The Decision for Internment

In December 1941, there were an estimated 120,000 persons of Japanese descent living in the Pacific coastal region of the United States. Approximately two thirds of this number were, in fact, American citizens. Despite persistent racial prejudice from much of the native white population, Japanese-American communities had grown and thrived on the west coast since the early 20th Century. Despite this population's embrace of their new country, there were many who feared that Japanese in America would become a "fifth column" on behalf of Japan in the event of war between the two countries.

At first, in the immediate aftermath of Pearl Harbor, there was no real momentum for internment of Japanese residents on the Pacific coast. However, as Japanese forces won victory after victory against American, British Commonwealth, and Dutch forces in the Far East, fear mounted of a possible Japanese attack on the west coast. Sadly, all too many Americans directed their anger over Japanese actions at their fellow citizens of Japanese descent. Unfounded rumors spread like wildfire, alleging widespread sabotage and espionage activities by Japanese-Americans on behalf of Tokyo. Racial prejudice further fueled such fears, as nativist groups exploited this overheated environment to demand the expulsion of Japanese-Americans from the Pacific coast. Finally, many newspapers and prominent west coast politicians, such as the mayor of Los Angeles, the governor of California, and numerous congressmen, joined the growing chorus demanding action against Japanese-Americans.

"Japanese-Americans with their baggage waiting for trains which will take them to Owens Valley." Los Angeles, April 1942. Library of Congress Prints & Photographs Division: http://www.loc.gov/pictures/resource/fsa.8a31159/

Federal authorities initially resisted these calls. Attorney General Francis Biddle resolutely opposed any form of mass internment, or incarceration based solely on race or national origin. The organizations directly responsible for coping with domestic pro-Axis subversion, the FBI, military intelligence, and naval intelligence, all insisted that internment was unnecessary and the problem of possible subversion among Japanese-Americans was well in hand.

Initially, the Army likewise opposed the deportation of persons of Japanese descent from the west coast. However, as the public outcry against Japanese-Americans grew, the commander of military forces along the Pacific coast, Lt. General John L. DeWitt, allowed himself to be persuaded of the necessity of mass internment. On February 14, 1942, DeWitt recommended that all Japanese-Americans, citizens and non-citizens, be removed from "sensitive areas." Bowing to both the recommendation of his general, and to the growing public hysteria, President Roosevelt on February 19, 1942, issued Executive Order No. 9066, which authorized the removal of all persons of Japanese descent from the western areas of California, Oregon, and Washington.

In all, some 117,000 Japanese-Americans were deported from the west coast during the spring of 1942. At first, they were encouraged to leave voluntarily, and to go anywhere else in the US that they wished. Starting in March, remaining Japanese residents were ordered to report to the authorities, and taken to government-run internment centers. Allowed to bring only what they could carry, many of the internees lost almost everything. Eventually, most deportees ended up in one of 10 major internment camps, most located in remote areas of the western US. These camps were run by an organization called the War Relocation Authority (WRA), which was part of the Interior Department. Japanese-Americans living elsewhere in the continental United States were not interned, nor were those living in Hawaii, despite their closer proximity to the theater of military operations.

The crude, racialist logic behind the mass internment of Japanese-Americans was clearly illustrated in comments made by General DeWitt. Testifying before a congressional subcommittee in April 1943, he defended his decision in the following terms:

> ...The danger of the Japanese was, and is now, -if they are permitted to come back- espionage and sabotage. It makes no difference whether he is an American citizen, he is still a Japanese. American citizenship does not necessarily determine loyalty. (Walker, "A Slap's a Slap")

As DeWitt infamously told the press, "a Jap's a Jap." No similar logic was applied to German-Americans or Italian-Americans.

HUAC Investigates Japanese-Americans

While the House Special Committee on Un-American Activities, which would become better known starting in 1945 as simply the House Un-American Activities Committee, played a relatively minor role in Japanese-American internment, the committee did support the decision. In particular, HUAC published several volumes and reports on the activities of Japanese "patriotic societies" that allegedly fostered loyalty to Tokyo at the expense of Washington (see list of sources below.)

HUAC's main contribution to the internment of Japanese-Americans was a series of public hearings focused on the internment facilities, in June-July, 1943 by a three-member subcommittee, consisting of Reps. John M. Costello (D-CA), Karl E. Mundt (R-SD), and Herman P. Eberharter (D-PA). On September 30, 1943, HUAC issued a report summarizing the results of this

Manzanar Relocation Center, California, 1943. Photograph by Ansel Adams. Manzanar War Relocation Center photographs, Library of Congress Prints and Photographs Division: http://www.loc.gov/pictures/collection/manz/item/2002695968/

investigation. Costello and Mundt, supported by the bulk of the committee, criticized the WRA for allowing the internment camps to become, in HUAC's view, hotbeds of pro-Tokyo subversion. Among other offenses, the committee condemned the WRA for permitting the teaching of judo and other Japanese cultural activities, which allegedly inhibited the inculcation of "positive Americanism" among the internees. Finally, the HUAC majority called for more rigorous efforts to separate loyal from disloyal internees, and demanded the implementation of a "thoroughgoing program of Americanization" in the camps. (*Establishment of the War Relocation Centers*, 8, 16)

Alone among HUAC's membership, Rep. Eberharter dissented strongly from this viewpoint. In a scathing critique published along with the majority report, Eberharter wrote that "I cannot avoid the conclusion that the report of the majority is prejudiced, and that most of its statements are not proven." (*Establishment of the War Relocation Centers*, 17) Rejecting the report's depiction of life in the camps, and its single-minded focus on subversion, Eberharter strongly defended the WRA against HUAC's charges. His comment on the Americanization proposal is especially telling, bitingly pointing out the absurdity behind it:

> Certainly, we would need an extraordinarily intensive Americanization program for loyal American citizens who are detained in seeming contradiction of American principles and the "four freedoms." (*Establishment of the War Relocation Centers*, 28)

Few statements so eloquently expressed how the countersubversive obsession at the heart of HUAC all too often made a mockery of the American ideals the committee claimed to defend.

Conclusion

Starting in 1943, Japanese-Americans gradually began to be released from the internment facilities. In December 1944, the Roosevelt Administration announced that all remaining internees would be freed. No credible evidence of widespread subversion or espionage among Japanese-Americans was ever found. In 1980, Congress created a commission to investigate the internment. Its report, released in December 1982, in many ways offers the final word on a sad chapter in American history:

> The promulgation of Executive Order 9066 was not justified by military necessity, and the decisions which followed from it....were not driven by analysis of military conditions. The broad historical causes which shaped these decisions were race prejudice, war hysteria and a failure of political leadership. Widespread ignorance of Japanese Americans contributed to a policy conceived in haste and executed in an atmosphere of fear and anger at Japan. A grave injustice was done to American citizens and resident aliens of Japanese ancestry who, without individual review or any probative evidence against them, were excluded, removed and detained by the United States during World War II. (*Personal Justice Denied*, 18)

In 1988, the Civil Liberties Act was passed by Congress and signed into law by President Reagan. This legislation condemned the internment of Japanese-Americans, and offered a presidential apology and financial compensation to the internees.

Soldiers of the 442nd Regimental Combat Team, US Army, June 1943.
Composed almost entirely of Japanese-Americans, the 442nd was the most heavily
decorated US Army unit of its size in World War II. Library of Congress Prints &
Photographs Division: https://www.loc.gov/pictures/item/00652071/

Congressional Sources on the Internment of Japanese-Americans

*Establishment of the War Relocation Centers: Report and Minority Views of
the Special Committee on Un-American Activities on Japanese War Relocation
Centers.* September 30, 1943.

*Investigation of Un-American Propaganda Activities in the United States:
Appendix VI: Report on Japanese Activities, Hearings before a Special Com-
mittee on Un-American Activities, House of Representatives, Seventy-Seventh
Congress, First Session.* 1942.

*Investigation of Un-American Propaganda Activities in the United States:
Appendix -Part VIII: Report on the Axis Front Movement in the United States:
Second Section -Japanese Activities, Hearings before a Special Committee on*

Un-American Activities, House of Representatives, Seventy-Eighth Congress, First Session. 1943.

Investigation of Un-American Propaganda Activities in the United States, Volume 15, Hearings before a Special Committee on Un-American Activities, House of Representatives, Seventy-Eighty Congress, First Session. June-July, 1943.

Investigation of Un-American Propaganda Activities in the United States, Volume 16, Hearings before a Special Committee on Un-American Activities, House of Representatives, Seventy-Eighty Congress, First Session. November-December, 1943.

War Relocation Centers. Hearings before a Subcommittee of the Committee on Military Affairs, United States Senate, Seventy-Eighth Congress, First Session. 4 vols. 1943–44.

Additional Federal Government Sources

Harry S. Truman Library and Museum. 'The War Relocation Authority & the Incarceration of Japanese-Americans During World War II.' https://www .trumanlibrary.gov/library/online-collections/war-relocation-authority -and-incarceration-of-japanese-americans.

Library of Congress. 'Japanese – Behind the Wire.' https://www.loc.gov /classroom-materials/immigration/japanese/behind-the-wire/.

Manzanar National Historic Site, Tule Lake Unit, National Park Service. 'A Brief History of Japanese American Relocation During World War II.' https://www .nps.gov/articles/historyinternment.htm.

National Archives and Records Administration. "Educator Resources: Japanese -American Incarceration During World War II." https://www.archives.gov /education/lessons/japanese-relocation.

National Archives and Records Administration. "Japanese American Internment." https://www.archives.gov/news/topics/japanese-american-internment.

National Archives and Records Administration. "Japanese Relocation and Internment." https://www.archives.gov/research/alic/reference/military /japanese-internment.html.

National Park Service, U.S. Department of the Interior. 'Japanese Americans in World War II.' A National Historic Landmark Theme Study (draft), February 2005. http://purl.fdlp.gov/GPO/gp073894.

Personal Justice Denied: Report of the Commission on Wartime Relocation and Internment of Civilians. 1983; 1992.

Unrau, Harlan D. Manzanar National Historic Site, *California: The Evacuation and Relocation of Persons of Japanese Ancestry during World War II: A Historical Study of the Manzanar War Relocation Center*. United States Department of the Interior, National Park Service, 1996.

Walker, Alan. "A Slap's a Slap: General John L. DeWitt and Four Little Words." *The Text Message Blog*, National Archives and Records Administration. https://text-message.blogs.archives.gov/2013/11/22/a-slaps-a-slap-general-john-l-dewitt-and-four-little-words/.

Further Sources

Adams, Ansel. *Born Free and Equal: Photographs of the Loyal Japanese-Americans at Manzanar Relocation Center, Inyo County, California*. New York: U.S. Camera, 1944.

Goodman, Walter. *The Committee: The Extraordinary Career of the House Committee on Un-American Activities*. New York: Farrar, Straus, and Giroux, 1968.

Grodzins, Morton. *Americans Betrayed: Politics and the Japanese Evacuation*. Chicago: University of Chicago Press, 1949.

Muller, Eric L. *American Inquisition: The Hunt for Japanese American Disloyalty in World War II*. Chapel Hill: University of North Carolina Press, 2007.

Myer, Dillon, S. *Uprooted Americans: The Japanese Americans and the War Relocation Authority during World War II*. Tucson: University of Arizona Press, 1971.

Stone, Geoffrey R *Perilous Times: Free Speech in Wartime from the Sedition Act of 1798 to the War on Terrorism*. New York: W.W. Norton & Co, 2004.

PART TWO

McCarthyism and Red Scare

1946–1959

Source for the Blacklist

The Origins of Appendix IX

Dr. Joseph B. (J.B.) Matthews, testifying before the Dies Committee in 1938.
Source: Harris & Ewing Collection, Library of Congress Prints and Photographs
Division: http://www.loc.gov/pictures/collection/hec/item/hec2009011686/

THE HOUSE UN-AMERICAN ACTIVITIES Committee went through a number of different phases in its long and controversial history. Having enjoyed a brief beginning in 1934–35, HUAC was reborn as the House Special Committee on Un-American Activities in 1938. Known as the Dies Committee after its chairman, Rep. Martin Dies, Jr. (D-TX), the committee made headlines as it investigated communist, Nazi, fascist and Japanese activities deemed subversive. The Dies Committee, and its chairman, placed a particular focus on pursuing communist and other radical left activities, examining such bodies as the Federal Theater Project and seeking to draw links between the Roosevelt Administration and New Deal and the Communist Party. In the words of historian Richard Gid Powers:

> The information the Committee collected in the thirties still forms the foundation for much of what we know today about communism in that decade. But the Committee really was not all that interested in simply collecting and publishing facts on the Communist Party and its activities. It was far more intent on using that information as ammunition for red-smearing attacks on the administration, attacks on the union movement, and attacks on unpopular opinions and associations. (Powers, *Not Without Honor*, 128)

This legacy would be embodied in the final act of the Dies Committee, the release of a publication that would provide much of the raw data used by self-appointed "red hunters" to determine candidates for blacklisting in the 1950s.

J.B. Matthews and Appendix IX

The individual most directly responsible for collecting the information used by the Dies Committee was its chief investigator, Dr. Joseph B. (J.B.) Matthews. A former Methodist missionary who held a divinity degree, Matthews turned to socialism in the early 1930s. He soon became what was known as a "fellow traveler," a non-communist who agreed with the communists on almost every issue and participated in numerous communist-led organizations. He had a falling out with the communists after a CPUSA-led strike at Consumers' Research, where Matthews was a top official. During the course of this strike, Matthews was publicly vilified by the CPUSA, an experience that turned him into a bitter opponent of the party.

Matthews testified before the Dies Committee in August 1938 as an expert witness on the CPUSA and its many front organizations, drawing on both his personal experiences and on a voluminous set of files he had begun to accumulate. Shortly afterwards, Dies hired Matthews to serve as the committee's chief researcher. "For the next six years," in the words of historian Robert M. Lichtman, "under Matthews's guidance, the committee directed its fire at alleged Communists and left-leaning New Deal officials, even during World War II when anti-communism was not in vogue." (Lichtman, "J. B. Matthews," 7)

By 1944, the Dies Committee was in serious political trouble. The committee's mandate was set to expire, and it looked likely that it would not be renewed. Dies himself, facing a serious political challenge from the Congress of Industrial Organizations' Political Action Committee (CIO-PAC), as well as health issues, decided in May that he would not run for reelection. In its final act, however, the committee would use J.B. Matthews's files to strike one last blow against CIO-PAC and its other opponents.

Late in 1944, fearing that the end of the committee meant that J.B. Matthews's voluminous files would disappear with it, a subcommittee of the Dies Committee authorized the official publication of Matthews's files as what became known as *Appendix IX*. Titled Communist Front Organizations, with Special Reference to the National Citizens Political Action Committee, the seven volume set numbered 2,138 pages. Only 7,000 sets were produced by the Government Printing Office, and these were distributed to a number of government agencies and private individuals. According to Lichtman, "The index to *Appendix IX* ... contained the names of 22,000 individuals and organizations—many Communist, many not. (Lichtman, "J. B. Matthews," 8)

Ironically enough, Matthews's fears for the safety of his files ultimately proved to be unnecessary. In early 1945, a parliamentary maneuver by Rep. John Rankin (D-MS) not only saved HUAC, but turned it into a permanent House committee. The newly-created HUAC, realizing the problems that could be caused by public access to "the raw and undifferentiated character of the information in *Appendix IX*," recalled the document. (Lichtman, "J. B. Matthews," 9) A few copies of *Appendix IX* survived, however, and in the hands of professional countersubversives soon became a key source of names for blacklisting within the entertainment industry.

Appendix IX

Investigation of Un-American Propaganda Activities in the United States. [Hearings] Seventy-Eighth Congress, Second Session on H. Res. 282. Appendix, Part IX: Communist Front Organizations, With Special Reference to the National Citizens Political Action Committee. 3 vols. 1944.

Additional Sources

Goodman, Walter. *The Committee: The Extraordinary Career of the House Committee on Un-American Activities.* New York: Farrar, Straus, and Giroux, 1968.

Lichtman, Robert M. "J. B. Matthews and the 'Countersubversives': Names as a Political and Financial Resource in the McCarthy Era." *American Communist History*, 5, 1 (2006): 1–36. DOI: 10.1080/14743890600763848.

Powers, Richard Gid. *Not Without Honor: The History of American Anticommunism.* New York: Free Press, 1995.

2

HUAC Goes to Hollywood, Aspects of the Blacklist

Rep. Martin Dies, Jr. (D-TX), chairman of the House Special Committee on Un-American Activities, February 17, 1940. That summer Dies, acting as a one-man subcommittee, would conduct HUAC's first investigation into communist activity in Hollywood. Library of Congress Prints & Photographs Division: https://www .loc.gov/resource/hec.28164/

Part 1: The Forgotten Investigation of 1940

The House Un-American Activities Committee launched three major investigations of communist influence in the motion picture industry. The most famous HUAC hearings regarding the film industry were the Hollywood Ten hearings of October 1947. In addition to numerous "friendly" witnesses such as Ronald Reagan, Gary Cooper, and Ayn Rand, HUAC subpoenaed 19 "unfriendly" witnesses believed to be tied to the Communist Party. Eleven testified before HUAC; ten openly defied the committee, and were eventually sentenced to up to a year in prison for contempt of Congress. These "Unfriendly Ten" eventually became known as the Hollywood Ten. In November 1947, the heads of the major Hollywood studios issued a statement that they would no longer employ the Ten, nor anyone else known to be a communist. This was the birth of the blacklist.

HUAC's final investigation of Hollywood occurred in 1951–52. By far the most extensive, this set of hearings featured nearly 100 witnesses. Those considered to be friendly witnesses "named names" of others they knew were part of the CPUSA; unfriendly witnesses pleaded the Fifth Amendment to avoid incriminating themselves and others.

The first investigation was the shortest, lasting only four days in the summer of 1940, and mostly being conducted behind closed doors. It remains little remembered today. It set the precedent, however, that the political leanings of Hollywood were a valid topic of congressional investigation, and paved the way for the far more extensive hearings of 1947 and 1951–52. The HUAC Hollywood investigation of 1940 was the first step on the road to the blacklist.

The Dies "Subcommittee" Goes to California

On July 17, 1940, Representative Martin Dies, Jr. (D-TX), chair of the House Special Committee on Un-American Activities, was taking testimony in Beaumont TX. as a one-man subcommittee. Among the witnesses was a man named John L. Leech. A former Communist party official in the Los Angeles area, Leech testified that 42 individuals involved in the motion picture industry were members of the CPUSA. Among the individuals he named was Fredric March, an Academy Award winner who was one of the major stars of the day. In a follow-up appearance before Dies on July 19, he named iconic actor James Cagney as another CPUSA member.

Fredric March (1897–1975), academy award winning actor, depicted on May 28,
1939. March was among the most prominent of those film industry personalities
summoned to testify before Martin Dies in August 1940. Library of Congress
Prints & Photographs Division, Carl Van Vechten Collection, [reproduction
number, e.g., LC-USZ62–54231]: https://www.loc.gov/item/2004663262/

While Leech's testimony was taken in executive session, meaning that it was behind closed doors, Dies released a summary that included Leech's broad claims about CPUSA influence in Hollywood, but without naming those implicated by Leech. However, many of the names were soon released by a Los Angeles grand jury that Leech also testified before. Having generated the press headlines he was seeking, Dies headed to California the next month to question some of the film industry personalities named by Leech.

Dies held four days of closed hearings in California: August 16–17 in Los Angeles, and August 19–20 in San Francisco. Again serving as a one-man subcommittee, Dies took testimony from a number of people associated with Hollywood, including Humphrey Bogart, Cagney, March, and screenwriter Philip Dunne. All denied being members or supporters of the CPUSA. Dies found their testimony convincing. Most of Leech's charges, in HUAC historian Walter Goodman's words, "dribbled away like sand." As soon as the hearings were over, Dies released a statement on August 20 absolving Bogart, March, Cagney, and Dunne of any ties to communism.

In the opinion of most writers, Dies' main goal in going to Hollywood seems to have been to generate publicity for himself and his committee. The Dies investigation itself had little impact on CPUSA efforts in Hollywood, or film industry political activism in general. The precedent Dies set, however, would have a far reaching impact. Just seven years later would come the infamous Hollywood Ten hearings, followed by the promulgation of the blacklist.

Primary Sources on the 1940 Hearings

Investigation of Un-American Propaganda Activities in the United States, Hearings before a Special Committee on Un-American Activities, House of Representatives, Seventy-Sixth Congress, Third Session. Volume 2, Executive Hearings. 1941.

Investigation of Un-American Propaganda Activities in the United States, Hearings before a Special Committee on Un-American Activities, House of Representatives, Seventy-Sixth Congress, Third Session. Volume 3, Executive Hearings. 1943.

Primary Sources on the Other HUAC Hollywood Hearings

Communist Infiltration of the Motion Picture Industry – Hearings before the Committee on Un-American Activities, House of Representatives, Eighty-Second Congress, First (Second) Session. 10 vols. 1951–52.

Hearings Regarding the Communist Infiltration of the Motion Picture Industry, Hearings before the Committee on Un-American Activities, House of Representatives, Eightieth Congress, First Session. 1947.

Additional Sources

Billingsley, Kenneth Lloyd. *Hollywood Party: How Communism Seduced the American Film Industry in the 1930s and 1940s.* Rocklin, CA: Prima Publishing, 1998.

Dunne, Philip. *Take Two: A Life in Movies and Politics.* New York: McGraw Hill, 1980.

Goodman, Walter. *The Committee: The Extraordinary Career of the House Committee on Un-American Activities.* New York: Farrar, Straus, and Giroux, 1968.

Radosh, Ronald, and Allis Radosh. *Red Star Over Hollywood: The Film Colony's Long Romance with the Left.* San Francisco: Encounter Books, 2005.

Part 2: Bible of the Blacklist

While the initial Hollywood blacklist, inaugurated in the wake of the 1947 Hollywood Ten hearings, was prompted by the efforts of the House Un-American Activities Committee, it was largely sustained by private businesses and pressure groups. Using information published by HUAC and other governmental investigative bodies, along with the results of their own research, a private-sector network of freelance "Red-hunters" emerged by the end of the 1940s. Working individually, in small consulting firms, or as part of larger pressure/advocacy organizations, these Red-hunters would produce evidence that many entertainment industry professionals were tied to the communist party. The persons they named would then either have to go through an elaborate clearance process, or find themselves blacklisted.

It would be one such small consulting business, founded by three former FBI agents, that in 1950 produced a volume that scholars call "the bible of the blacklist."

ABC and the Origins of Red Channels

In 1944, HUAC published its voluminous files on organizations believed tied to the CPUSA in a three volume compilation called *Appendix IX*. This set included the text of numerous committee lists, petitions, endorsements,

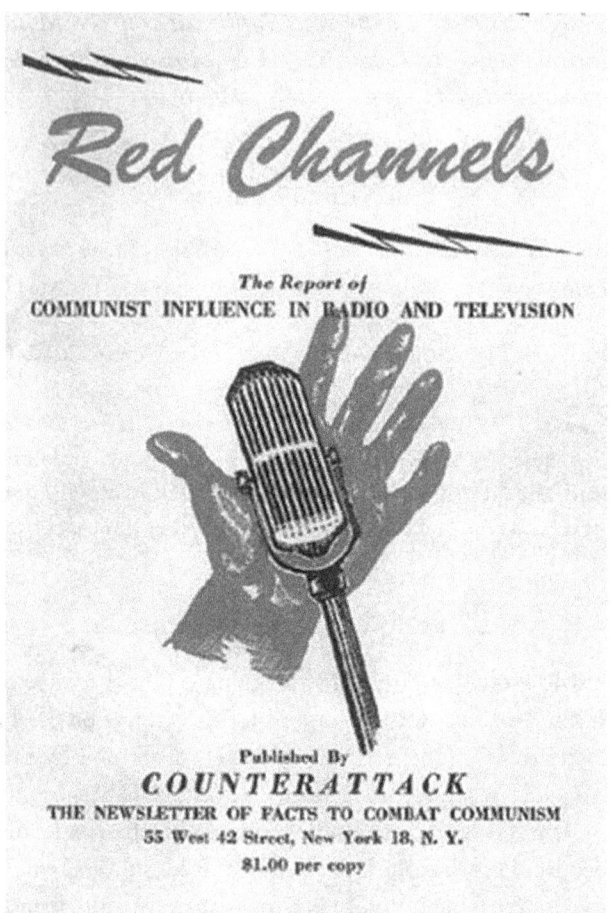

The front cover of Red Channels, published on June 22, 1950. Image from Wikimedia Commons via NPR: https://www.npr.org/templates/story/story.php?storyId=128005395

and other documentation of political activities. In all, *Appendix IX* contained the names of over 22,000 individuals, many of whom had little or no real connection to the CPUSA. *Appendix IX* was published out of fear that HUAC would not be renewed by the next congress, and thus this material would be lost. After HUAC was made a permanent body in early 1945, the committee realized the danger caused by publishing such a large amount of raw information containing so many individual names, and withdrew the document from publication. Some copies would survive, however, and become a major source of names for the blacklist.

In the spring of 1947, three former FBI agents, Kenneth Brierly, Theodore Kirkpatrick, and John Keenan, formed American Business Consultants (ABC), a small firm that researched, and published information on, communist activity in American society. Their periodical, Counterattack, eventually became a major source of names for studio blacklisters. In 1950, ABC hired a former naval intelligence officer named Vincent Hartnett to help with their research. On June 22, 1950, ABC published the fruits of Hartnett's research, a volume entitled *Red Channels: The Report of Communist Influence in Radio and Television.*

Drawing heavily on *Appendix IX* and other HUAC publications, *Red Channels* alleged that 151 professional entertainers were involved in communist activity. Those listed in *Red Channels* soon found themselves added to the blacklist, and found it virtually impossible to obtain work in radio or television. *Red Channels* became an indispensable source for blacklisters. Relying on information from it and other sources, groups such as the American Legion enforced the blacklist through boycotts and picketing. To have themselves removed, blacklistees had to undergo a lengthy "clearance" process, which involved renouncing communism and testifying before HUAC or a similar congressional body. The freelance "Red-hunters" at ABC and elsewhere offered their services to guide repentant blacklistees through this process, often for a fee.

With the publication of *Red Channels*, Hartnett found himself considered an expert on the topic of alleged communist infiltration of the entertainment industry. He would make several appearances before HUAC and related congressional committees. The blacklist his work helped fuel would reach its height by the mid-1950s.

Primary Sources

American Business Consultants, Inc. *Counterattack*, 13 (1959).

American Business Consultants, Inc. *Red Channels: The Report of Communist Influence in Radio and Television.* New York: Counterattack, 1950.

Cogley, John. *Report on Blacklisting: II – Radio – Television.* New York: Fund for the Republic, 1956.

Investigation of Un-American Propaganda Activities in the United States.
[Hearings] Seventy-Eighth Congress, Second Session on H. Res. 282. Appendix,
Part IX: Communist Front Organizations, With Special Reference to the Natio-
nal Citizens Political Action Committee. 3 vols. 1944.
Subversive Infiltration of Radio, Television and the Entertainment industry:
Hearings Before the Subcommittee to Investigate the Administration of the
Internal Security Act and Other Internal Security Laws of the Committee on
the Judiciary, United States Senate, Eighty-Second Congress, First and Second
sessions. 2 pts. 1952.

Additional Sources

Hill, Jason. *Red Channels: The Bible of Blacklisting.* Albany, GA: BearManor
   Media, 2016.
McDonough, John. "Reliving The Scare: Looking Back On 'Red Channels'."
   NPR, June 22, 2010. https://www.npr.org/templates/story/story.php?storyId
   =128005395.
Powers, Richard Gid. *Not Without Honor: The History of American*
   Anticommunism. New York: Free Press, 1995.
Schrecker, Ellen. *The Age of McCarthyism: A Brief History with Documents.*
   2nd ed. Boston: Bedford/St. Martin's, 2002.

Part 3: Investigating the Blacklist's Critics

While the blacklist was inaugurated in November 1947, in the immediate
aftermath of the House Un-American Activities Committee's infamous
Hollywood Ten hearings, it was not until the early 1950s that it became
truly widespread. The June 1950 publication of *Red Channels* catalyzed the
spread of the blacklist to radio and television. In hearings from 1951–53,
HUAC identified 324 people associated with Hollywood as being involved with the communist party. 212 of these people were still part of the
motion-picture business, and HUAC's publication of their names made it
almost impossible for them to find work without first undergoing a lengthy
clearance process.

While HUAC was not directly involved with the blacklist, its hearings
and other publications served as ammunition for the advocacy and pressure
organizations that enforced it. HUAC even weighed in against those who
criticized the blacklist, most notably in the summer of 1956.

Robert Maynard Hutchins (1899–1977), long-time
president of the University of Chicago and chairman of the
Fund for the Republic. Image via University of Chicago.
Source: https://president.uchicago.edu/directory
/robert-maynard-hutchins

The Fund for the Republic and The *Report on Blacklisting*

By the early 1950s, the blacklist had come under criticism even from mainstream Cold War liberals. They saw the blacklist, as well as the broader climate of suspicion and subversive-hunting, as a grave threat to civil liberties. In 1952, a number of notable liberals, including Robert Maynard Hutchins, former president of the University of Chicago, founded The Fund for the Republic. The Fund described itself as "an educational undertaking in the field of civil liberties in the United States."

The Fund began an extensive investigation of the blacklist in September 1954. They set up a special research team under John Cogley, editor of the Catholic publication *Commonweal*. Cogley's team completed their work by the end of 1955. On June 24, 1956, the Fund published the results of this effort, the two-volume *Report on Blacklisting*. The report discusses the workings and impact of the blacklist in great detail, clearly outlining the role played by ABC, *Red Channels,* and *Counterattack*.

Even before the *Report on Blacklisting* was published, the Fund's investigation drew the ire of HUAC, and of those individuals and organizations who enforced the blacklist. There were even rumblings of taking away the Fund's tax-exempt status. In June, HUAC announced that it would hold hearings investigating the Fund for the Republic. These hearings began on July 10, 1956. John Cogley was the first witness.

For over three hours, the committee grilled Cogley regarding his sources, methods, and conclusions. Among other things, he was challenged over the presence of democratic socialist Michael Harrington on his research staff. At one point, a frustrated Cogley responded by saying "I did not anticipate congressional investigation of the book I was about to write." (*Investigation of So-Called "Blacklisting", pt. 1*, 5210) The tone of his testimony was summarized in Cogley's 1973 *New York Times* obituary:

> Mr. Cogley, who declined to have a lawyer at his side on the ground that "I didn't see why I had to have anybody on hand to protect my rights before a group of Congressmen," refused to discuss confidential sources and reportedly came close to a contempt citation. Public opinion was generally on his side, however, and no action was taken against him. (Fiske, "John Cogley Dies at 60")

In all, HUAC held six days of hearings on the *Report on Blacklisting*. After Cogley finished his testimony, most subsequent witnesses were defenders of the blacklist, such as *Red Channels* author Vincent Hartnett.

The Fund for the Republic hearings stand out as a particularly egregious example of HUAC abusing its authority to threaten the right to free expression. While the hearings may have had a short-term chilling effect on critics of the blacklist, the tide was already beginning to turn. In 1960, former communist and Hollywood Ten member Dalton Trumbo was openly credited as the screenwriter for the films *Exodus* and *Spartacus*, moves that heralded the beginning of the end of the blacklist.

While not without its flaws, the *Report on Blacklisting* remains an essential source on this controversial episode of American history.

Primary Sources

Annual Report of the Committee on Un-American Activities for the Year 1952. Washington D.C.: Government Printing Office, 1953.
Annual Report of the Committee on Un-American Activities for the Year 1953. Washington D.C.: Government Printing Office, 1954.

Cogley, John. *Report on Blacklisting: I – Movies*. New York: Fund for the Republic, 1956.

Cogley, John. *Report on Blacklisting: II – Radio – Television*. New York: Fund for the Republic, 1956.

Investigation of So-Called "Blacklisting" in Entertainment Industry: Report of the Fund for the Republic, Inc. – Part 1. Hearings before the Committee on Un-American Activities, House of Representatives, Eighty-Fourth Congress, Second Session. 1956.

Investigation of So-Called "Blacklisting" in Entertainment Industry: Report of the Fund for the Republic, Inc. – Part 2. Hearings before the Committee on Un-American Activities, House of Representatives, Eighty-Fourth Congress, Second Session. 1956.

Investigation of So-Called "Blacklisting" in Entertainment Industry: Report of the Fund for the Republic, Inc. – Part 3. Hearings before the Committee on Un-American Activities, House of Representatives, Eighty-Fourth Congress, Second Session. 1956.

Tax-exempt Foundations: Hearings before the Special Committee to Investigate Tax-Exempt Foundations and Comparable Organizations, House of Representatives, Eighty-Third Congress, Second Session, on H. Res. 217. 1954, 2 pts.

Tax-exempt Foundations: Report of the Special Committee to Investigate Tax-Exempt Foundations and Comparable Organizations, House of Representatives, Eighty-Third Congress, Second Session, on H. Res. 217. 1954.

Additional Sources

Fiske, Edward B. "John Cogley Dies at 60; Expert on Catholicism." *New York Times*, March 30, 1976. https://www.nytimes.com/1976/03/30/archives/john-cogley-dies-at-60–expert-on-catholicism.html.

Reeves, Thomas C. *Freedom and the Foundation: The Fund for the Republic in the Era of McCarthyism*. New York: Knopf, 1969.

Part 4: All the Party's Men

Robert Rossen (1908–1966) was a Hollywood film director and former communist party member, who on two occasions was called to testify before the House Committee on Un-American Activities. His controversial film *All the King's Men*, released at the end of 1949, would go on to win the Academy Award for Best Picture. It is perhaps then, not a surprise that Rossen would be subjected to a strenuous ideological interrogation over the content of his film. Nor is it surprising that the ten "unfriendly" 1947 HUAC witnesses known as the Hollywood Ten would be present at this event. What will likely come as a surprise is that it was not HUAC, but the Hollywood Ten themselves who served as Rossen's inquisitors.

The Communist Party and Artistic Freedom

The entertainment industry blacklist imposed on those suspected of CPUSA involvement or sympathies began to fade by the late 1950s, and was all but over by the mid-1960s. Today, the blacklist is justifiably seen as a grave assault on civil liberties and artistic freedom. The specter of a congressional committee working in tandem with private organizations and activists to deny employment to individuals based on their political views is quite disturbing. Those who resisted HUAC and the blacklist are often seen as uncompromising defenders of intellectual freedom, while those who agreed to "name names" are derided as cowards or sellouts.

There is however, a complicating factor involved. Many of those blacklisted, including all the Hollywood Ten, were at some point involved with the CPUSA. The party demanded that its members uphold what was known as the "party line" under all circumstances. Committed to upholding that line, many of them saw artistic freedom and civil liberties as tools to be used only in support of the CPUSA, not against it. The CPUSA forbade its members from reading books that were critical of communism or the USSR, and actively campaigned against films deemed "reactionary." It demanded intellectual freedom and civil liberties for its supporters, while calling for those same rights to be denied to its opponents. Most infamously, in 1949, the pro-CPUSA actor/singer Paul Robeson spoke at a rally where he denounced the federal government's prosecution of CPUSA leaders. At the same event, in response to a question, he defended the prosecution of Trotskyists, the CPUSA's archenemies, under the same statute being used against the communists. Robeson justified his view by comparing Trotskyists to the Klan and argued that "Would you give civil rights to the Ku Klux Klan?" (Quoted in Duberman, *Paul Robeson*, 382)

Among Hollywood communists, the CPUSA sought to force its members to subordinate their art to the party line. These demands for ideological conformity drove a number of writers and directors to quit the party.

Screenwriter and novelist Budd Schulberg, for example, left the CPUSA after being pressured to alter his 1940 novel *What Makes Sammy Run* to suit the dictates of the party. Schulberg's friend, director Elia Kazan would later leave the party over similar concerns. Both would eventually become "friendly" witnesses before HUAC.

Even the Hollywood Ten themselves were subject to the party's ideological censorship. Edward Dmytryk, the one member of the Ten who would ultimately become a "friendly" witness, was expelled from the CPUSA in 1945 for refusing to make changes to his film *Cornered* that the party demanded. Others, such as Albert Maltz, caved in to the party's dictates. In February 1946, Maltz published an essay in the party literary journal *New Masses* titled "What Shall We Ask of Writers." Maltz argues that art should not be seen merely as a vehicle for politics, but should be judged on its own merits. For nearly two months, Maltz was pilloried for this view by his fellow communists. Finally, in April, Maltz gave in and returned to the party fold, publishing a second New Masses piece in which he retracted his earlier views.

Rossen, the Party, and *All the King's Men*

Rossen had joined the CPUSA in 1937, but had become disillusioned by the late 1940s. *All the King's Men*, with its strong theme of power corrupting, was deemed antithetical to the party line, possibly a thinly-veiled attack on Stalin himself, something anathema to the CPUSA. Still a party member, Rossen was summoned, ironically, to Albert Maltz's house, where the Hollywood Ten waited as an ideological board of inquiry. According to Dmytryk, after much heated discussion, Rossen finally told his inquisitors to "Stick the whole party up your ass!" before walking out in disgust. (Quoted in Dmytryk, *Odd Man Out*, 115) Dmytryk's account is confirmed by comments made by Ring Lardner, Jr., another of the Ten: "There was a similar discussion...about the movie *All the King's Men*, with Robert Rossen...and there again the result of the discussion was to drive Rossen out of the Party." (Quoted in Schwartz, *The Hollywood Writers' Wars*, 170; cited in Neve, "Red Hollywood in Transition," 196)

Rossen would testify twice before HUAC. In 1951, he pleaded the Fifth Amendment, but in 1953, he appeared as a friendly witness. Factors such as financial hardship, career considerations, and personal animus, certainly played a major role in why many "friendly" witnesses chose to name names.

However, the belief that the CPUSA itself posed a threat to artistic freedom, and that it did the bidding of a hostile foreign power in the USSR, was also a factor in persuading many such as Rossen to testify.

Primary Sources

Communist Infiltration of the Motion Picture Industry – Part 3, Hearings before the Committee on Un-American Activities, House of Representatives, Eighty-Second Congress, First Session. 1951.

Investigation of Communist Activities in the New York City Area – Part 4. Hearing before the Committee on Un-American Activities, House of Representatives, Eighty-Third Congress, First Session. 1953.

Maltz, Albert. "What Shall We Ask of Writers," *New Masses,* 58 (February 12, 1946).

Maltz, Albert. "Moving Forward," *New Masses,* 58 (April 9, 1946).

Additional Sources

Billingsley, Kenneth Lloyd. *Hollywood Party: How Communism Seduced the American Film Industry in the 1930s and 1940s.* Rocklin, CA: Prima Publishing, 1998.

Casty, Alan. *Communism in Hollywood: The Moral Paradoxes of Testimony, Silence, and Betrayal.* Lanham, MD: Scarecrow Press, 2009.

Casty, Alan. *Robert Rossen: The Films and Politics of a Blacklisted Idealist.* Jefferson, NC; London: McFarland & Company, Inc., Publishers, 2013.

Dmytryk, Edward. *Odd Man Out: A Memoir of the Hollywood Ten.* Carbondale, Il: Southern Illinois University Press, 1996.

Duberman, Martin Bauml. *Paul Robeson.* New York: Knopf, 1988.

McGilligan, Patrick, and Paul Buhle. *Tender Comrades: A Backstory of the Hollywood Blacklist.* Minneapolis: University of Minnesota Press, 2012.

Neve, Brian. "Red Hollywood in Transition: The Case of Robert Rossen." in *"Un-American" Hollywood: Politics and Film in the Blacklist Era.* ed. Frank Krutnik, et al. New Brunswick, N.J.: Rutgers University Press, 2007, 184–197.

Radosh, Ronald, and Allis Radosh. *Red Star Over Hollywood: The Film Colony's Long Romance with the Left.* San Francisco: Encounter Books, 2005.

Schwartz, Nancy Lynn, and Sheila Schwartz. *The Hollywood Writers' Wars.* New York: Knopf, 1982.

3

Jackie Robinson Testifies Before HUAC, 1949

Front cover of July 1951 comic book featuring Jackie Robinson.
Source: Library of Congress American Memory Collections:
Baseball and Jackie Robinson: http://memory.loc.gov/
ammem/collections/robinson/

I N 1947, JACK ROOSEVELT "Jackie" Robinson would make American history as the first African-American to officially play Major League Baseball
in the 20th Century. On July 18 1949, his status as a hero would see Jackie
Robinson summoned to testify before the House Un-American Activities
Committee.

HUAC was holding hearings on the topic of "Communist infiltration
of minority groups". In April 1949, the radical African-American singer and
actor Paul Robeson had allegedly stated that African-Americans would be
reluctant to fight on behalf of the USA against the USSR. Robinson was
invited by the committee as a "friendly" witness to rebut Robeson's claims.

Robinson began his testimony by stating that "it isn't exactly pleasant to
get involved in a political dispute", but that he decided ultimately to testify
out of "a sense of responsibility." While noting that "I don't pretend to be
any expert on communism or any other kind of a political 'ism.'" Robinson
pointed out that he was "an expert at being a colored American, with 30 years
of experience at it." After reminding the committee that he was still one of
only seven African-Americans in Major League Baseball (out of 400 players),
Robinson made a powerful statement about both African-Americans' desire
for civil rights and the tendency fostered by HUAC to see all social protest
as a result of conspiratorial subversion:

> The white public should start toward real understanding by apprecia-
> ting that every single Negro who is worth his salt is going to resent any
> kind of slurs and discrimination because of his race, and he is going to
> use every bit of intelligence such as he has to stop it. This has got abso-
> lutely nothing to do with what Communists may or may not be trying
> to do. And white people must realize that the more a Negro hates com-
> munism because it opposes democracy, the more he is going to hate any
> other influence that kills off democracy in this country-and that goes for
> racial discrimination in the Army, and segregation on trains and buses,
> and job discrimination because of religious beliefs or color or place of
> birth.
>
>   And one other thing the American public ought to understand, if we
> are to make progress in this matter: The fact that it is a Communist who
> denounces injustice in the courts, police brutality, and lynching when
> it happens doesn't change the truth of his charges. Just because Com-
> munists kick up a big fuss over racial discrimination when it suits their

purposes, a lot of people try to pretend that the whole issue is a creation of Communist imagination.

But they are not fooling anyone with this kind of pretense, and talk about "Communists stirring up Negroes to protest" only makes present misunderstanding worse than ever. Negroes were stirred up long before there was a Communist Party, and they'll stay stirred up long after the party has disappeared-unless Jim Crow has disappeared by then as well. (*Hearings Regarding*, 481)

Primary Source

Hearings Regarding Communist Infiltration of Minority Groups–Part 1, Hearings Before the Committee on Un-American Activities, House of Representatives, Eighty First Congress, First Session. 1949.

Additional Sources on Jackie Robinson

National Archives. "Jackie Robinson, Civil Rights Advocate." https://www .archives.gov/education/lessons/jackie-robinson.

4

New Evidence in the Case of J. Robert Oppenheimer

Dr. J. Robert Oppenheimer (1904-1967), widely considered to be the father of
the atomic bomb. Suspected of communist ties, his security clearance was revoked
in 1954. Source: Breaking Through: A Century of Physics at Berkeley, Bancroft
Library, University of California, Berkeley. http://bancroft.berkeley.edu
/Exhibits/physics/bigscienceo3.html

ONE OF THE GREATEST controversies concerning Cold War internal security measures is the case of Dr. J. Robert Oppenheimer. One of the greatest nuclear physicists of the 20th Century, Oppenheimer was one of the leading scientists involved in the Manhattan Project that created the atomic bomb during World War II. After the war, he remained a key figure in U.S. nuclear research. However, by the early 1950s, suspicions concerning Oppenheimer's past involvement with the communist party, as well as disagreements with some of his positions on future development of nuclear weapons, led many both within and outside the U.S. government to consider Oppenheimer a security risk.

In December 1953, the U.S. Atomic Energy Commission suspended Oppenheimer's security clearance, thus preventing him from engaging in nuclear research. In April-May 1954, the commission convened a three member personnel security board, which held a series of closed-door hearings to consider the case against Oppenheimer. At the conclusion of the hearings, the board voted two-to-one to permanently remove Oppenheimer's clearance. In the words of Department of Energy (DOE) historian Terry Fehner, "The board found Oppenheimer loyal and discreet but nevertheless a security risk." On June 28, the Atomic Energy Commission voted four-to-one to confirm the board's recommendation and permanently revoke Robert Oppenheimer's security clearance.

The Oppenheimer case has been a source of great controversy ever since. Almost all historians agree that Oppenheimer had nothing to do with Soviet espionage against the Manhattan Project. Divisions remain, however, on the extent of his involvement with the CPUSA. It is commonly accepted that both Oppenheimer's wife, and his brother Frank, were CPUSA members. Whether Robert Oppenheimer himself was a party member is still disputed. Many Oppenheimer biographers, such as Kai Bird and Martin J. Sherwin, maintain that he was merely a "fellow traveler" who supported the party and shared many of its causes. John Earl Haynes and Harvey Klehr, however, argue that Oppenheimer was indeed a CPUSA member from 1939-1942, but that he left the party and abandoned communism upon joining the Manhattan Project in 1942.

In June 1954, the Atomic Energy Commission published an unclassified, one volume transcript of the Oppenheimer personnel security board hearings. The rest of the hearings remained classified until very recently. However, in October 2014, the Department of Energy finally published the entire transcript of the hearings, in 19 volumes made available on the DOE website. In an October 11 overview of the newly released transcripts, the New York Times cited the verdict of scholars that the new Oppenheimer material "offers no damning evidence against him, and that the testimony that has been kept secret all these years tends to exonerate him."

Addendum

On December 16, 2022 Secretary of Energy Jennifer Granholm officially vacated the 1954 decision to revoke Oppenheimer's security clearance.

The Oppenheimer Hearing Documents

U.S. Department of Energy. "Secretary Granholm Statement on DOE Order Vacating 1954 Atomic Energy Commission Decision In the Matter of J. Robert Oppenheimer." December 16, 2022. https://www.energy.gov/articles/secretary-granholm-statement-doe-order-vacating-1954-atomic-energy-commission-decision.

U.S. Atomic Energy Commission. *In the matter of J. Robert Oppenheimer: Texts of Principal Documents and Letters of Personnel Security Board, General Manager, Commissioners, Washington, D.C. May 27, 1954 through June 29, 1954.* Washington, D.C.: Government Printing Office: 1954.

U.S. Atomic Energy Commission. *In the matter of J. Robert Oppenheimer: Transcript of Hearing Before Personnel Security Board, Washington D.C., April 12, 1954, through May 6, 1954.* Washington, D.C.: Government Printing Office: 1954.

U.S. Atomic Energy Commission. "J. Robert Oppenheimer Personnel Hearings Transcripts." U.S. Department of Energy, 2014. https://www.osti.gov/opennet/hearing.

Other Primary Documents Related to J. Robert Oppenheimer

Hearings Regarding Communist Infiltration of Radiation Laboratory and Atomic Bomb Project at the University of California, Berkeley, Calif – Vol. I (Including Foreward). Hearings Before the Committee on Un-American Activities, House of Representatives, Eighty-First Congress, First Session. 1949.

Hearings Regarding Communist Infiltration of Radiation Laboratory and Atomic Bomb Project at the University of California, Berkeley, Calif – Vol. II (Identification of Scientist X). Hearings Before the Committee on Un-American Activities, House of Representatives, Eighty-First Congress, First Session. 1949.

Hearings Regarding Communist Infiltration of Radiation Laboratory and Atomic Bomb Project at the University of California, Berkeley, Calif – Volume Three. Hearings Before the Committee on Un-American Activities, House of Representatives, Eighty-First Congress, Second Session. 1950.

Testimony of Dr. Edward U. Condon. Hearing Before the Committee on Un-American Activities, House of Representatives, Eighty-Second Congress, Second Session. 1952.

Additional Sources

Bird, Kai and Martin J. Sherwin. *American Prometheus: The Triumph and Tragedy of J. Robert Oppenheimer.* New York: Alfred A. Knopf, 2005.

Broad, William J. 'Transcripts Kept Secret for 60 Years Bolster Defense of Oppenheimer's Loyalty." *New York Times*, October 11, 2014. https://www.nytimes.com/2014/10/12/us/transcripts-kept-secret-for-60-years-bolster-defense-of-oppenheimers-loyalty.html.

Fehner, Terry. 'Unlocking the Mysteries of the J. Robert Oppenheimer Transcript.' *Breaking Energy* (blog), October 8, 2014. https://breakingenergy.com/2014/10/08/unlocking-the-mysteries-of-the-j-robert-oppenheimer-transcript/.

Haynes, John Earl and Harvey Klehr. 'J. Robert Oppenheimer: A Spy? No. But a Communist Once? Yes.' *Washington Decoded*, February 11, 2012. https://www.washingtondecoded.com/site/2012/02/jro.html.

Haynes, John Earl, Harvey Klehr and Alexander Vassiliev. *Spies: The Rise and Fall of the KGB in America.* New Haven: Yale University Press, 2009.

Pais, Abraham and Robert P. Crease. *J. Robert Oppenheimer: A Life.* New York: Oxford University Press, 2006.

Thorpe, Charles. *Oppenheimer: The Tragic Intellect.* Chicago: University of Chicago Press, 2006.

5

"Have you left no sense of decency"

The Army-McCarthy Hearings, 1954

J UNE 9, 1954 SAW one of the most iconic moments in 20th Century American politics, the televised confrontation that marked both the beginning of the end of one of the controversial politicians in American history, as well as the instant when, in the words of author Robert Shogan, "television became the dominant force in American politics." This was when a Boston lawyer named Joseph Welch would rebuke Senator Joseph R. McCarthy (R-WI) with a phrase that would resonate in American culture down to the present day, defining for many the negative side of countersubversive anti-communism.

The Rise of Joe McCarthy

McCarthy, elected to the Senate in 1946 after serving as a Marine intelligence officer in World War II, would first make his name as a "red-hunter" in February 1950. That month, McCarthy gave a blockbuster speech in Wheeling, WV, alleging widespread communist infiltration of the U.S. State Department. The resulting firestorm of controversy made McCarthy a national figure, revered by many countersubversive anti-communists, but hated by many moderates and liberals.

McCarthy thrived on the notoriety. He would remain in the news by making numerous charges of communist sympathies and even Soviet espionage against current and former officials in the State and Defense departments. On June 14, 1951, McCarthy made his infamous "a conspiracy so immense" speech, in which he viciously attacked the former Army Chief of Staff and Secretary of State George C. Marshall. "Without putting it in so many words," as historian David M. Oshinsky put it, McCarthy "called the general a traitor to his country." (Oshinsky, *A Conspiracy so Immense*, 200)

McCarthy vs. the Army

McCarthy would reach the pinnacle of his power in 1953. With Republicans winning a Senate majority in the 1952 congressional elections, McCarthy assumed the chairmanship of the Senate Committee on Government Operations and its Permanent Subcommittee on Investigations (SPSI). As Chair of SPSI, McCarthy now had an institutional platform from which to launch investigations of real and alleged communists in the U.S. government.

After investigating such agencies as the Voice of America and the Government Printing Office, McCarthy and SPSI soon focused on the U.S. Army as a suitable target. SPSI launched inquiries of suspected disloyalty among Army civilian workers, as well as among servicemen at the Army Signal Corps facility at Ft. Monmouth, NJ. These investigations led to an increasingly bitter confrontation between Senator McCarthy and the Army, punctuated by the Wisconsin senator's angry grilling of Brigadier General Ralph Zwicker at a hearing in February 1954. In March, the Army demanded that McCarthy fire his lead counsel, Roy Cohn, or else they would release a dossier documenting Cohn's demands that the Army grant favorable treatment to David Schine, a McCarthy staffer drafted into the Army the previous year. McCarthy refused, and the Army released the dossier on March 11, 1954. McCarthy responded by accusing the Army of trying to blackmail him and otherwise obstruct SPSI's efforts to investigate Army security lapses.

The Army-McCarthy Hearings

In the wake of this controversy, Senator McCarthy stepped down as Chair of SPSI. The subcommittee decided to conduct its own, public investigation of the "charges and countercharges" between McCarthy and the Army. As a party to the controversy, McCarthy was not allowed to sit on the subcommittee, but was permitted to attend and cross-examine witnesses. The Army's appointed counsel, a Boston lawyer named Joseph Nye Welch, was given the same privileges. The hearings, which were televised live, began on April 22, 1954.

Over the course of the hearings, McCarthy found himself increasingly frustrated by the seemingly mild-mannered Welch. In Shogan's words, McCarthy "endured Welch's well-bred, taunting voice, his cultured sarcasm, his grating fondness for self-deprecation. And all the while the senator saw his own reputation ... slowly crumbling away." McCarthy's frustrations came to a head on June 9th. In the middle of Welch's questioning of Roy Cohn, the senator from Wisconsin interjected to note that a young lawyer in Welch's law firm, Fred Fisher, had once been a member of the communist-affiliated National Lawyers' Guild. This despite the fact that Welch had made a deal with Roy Cohn not to bring up Fisher in return for not referring to Cohn's draft deferrals, a deal that McCarthy had approved:

> Senator MCCARTHY. Not exactly, Mr. Chairman, but in view of Mr. Welch's request that the information be given once we know of anyone who might be performing any work for the Communist Party, I think we should tell him that he has in his law firm a young man named Fisher whom he recommended, incidentally, to do work on this committee, who has been for a number of years a member of an organization which was named, oh, years and years ago, as the legal bulwark of the Communist Party, an organization which always swings to the defense of anyone who dares to expose Communists. (*Special Senate Investigation*, pt. 59, 2426–2427)

Welch's devastating response to McCarthy's heavy-handed maneuver would become one of the most memorable quotes in American political history:

> Let us not assassinate this lad further. Senator. You have done enough. Have you no sense of decency, sir, at long last? Have you left no sense of decency? (*Special Senate Investigation*, pt. 59, 2429)

This exchange has come to epitomize McCarthy's brazenly confrontational style of public debate, what Oshinsky has described as "his windy speeches, his endless interruptions, his frightening outbursts. his crude personal attacks." (Oshinsky, *A Conspiracy so Immense*, 464) It marked the culmination of a months-long decline in McCarthy's popularity.

The Army-McCarthy hearings concluded on June 17, 1954. Their main impact was to deal an irreparable blow to McCarthy's prestige and popularity. The Senate would vote to censure McCarthy in December 1954, after which the senator from Wisconsin faded from the headlines until his death in 1957. His name would become a byword for all the excesses of the post WWII campaign against domestic communism.

Primary Sources

Army Signal Corps – Subversion and Espionage. Hearings before the Permanent Subcommittee on Investigations of the Committee on Government Operations, United States Senate, Eighty-Third Congress, First (-Second) Session, pursuant to S. Res. 189. 11 pts. 1953–54.

Communist Infiltration Among Army Civilian Workers. Hearing before the Permanent Subcommittee on Investigations of the Committee on Government Operations, United States Senate, Eighty-Third Congress, First Session, pursuant to S. Res. 189. 1953.

Communist Infiltration in the Army. Hearings before the Permanent Subcommittee on Investigations of the Committee on Government Operations, United States Senate, Eighty-Third Congress, First (-Second) Session, pursuant to S. Res. 189. 4 pts. 1953–54.

Executive Sessions of the Senate Permanent Subcommittee on Investigations of the Committee on Government Operations. 5 vols. + index. 1953–54. *Washington, D.C.: Government Printing Office,* 2003.

Hearings on S. Res. 301. Hearings before a Select Committee to Study Censure Charges, United States Senate, Eighty-Third Congress, Second Session, pursuant to the order on S. Res. 301 and amendments. 2 pts. 1954.

Special Senate Investigation on Charges and Countercharges Involving: Secretary of the Army Robert T. Stevens, John G. Adams, H. Struve Hensel and Senator Joe McCarthy, Roy M. Cohn, and Francis P. Carr. Hearings before the Special Subcommittee on Investigations of the Committee on Government Operations, United States Senate, Eighty-Third Congress, Second Session, pursuant to S. Res. 189. 71 pts. + index. 1954.

State Department Employee Loyalty Investigation. Hearings before a Subcommittee of the Committee on Foreign Relations, United States Senate, Eighty-First Congress, Second Session, pursuant to S. Res. 231. 3 pts. 1950.

Additional Sources

Morgan, Ted. *Reds: McCarthyism in Twentieth-Century America.* New York: Random House, 2003.

Oshinsky, David M. *A Conspiracy so Immense: The World of Joe McCarthy.* New York: Free Press, 1983.

Shogan, Robert. *No Sense of Decency: The Army-McCarthy Hearings: A Demagogue Falls and Television Takes Charge of American Politics.* Chicago: Ivan R. Dee, 2009.

6

Pete Seeger and HUAC, 1955

Pete Seeger arrives at a Federal courthouse for sentencing with his banjo over his shoulder, April 4, 1961. Seeger had been convicted of contempt of Congress on March 29 for his refusal to cooperate with HUAC in 1955. Seeger was sentenced to a year in prison, but his conviction was overturned on appeal the following year. Source: New York World-Telegram and the Sun Newspaper Photograph Collection, Library of Congress Prints and Photographs Division: http://www.loc.gov/pictures/item/2002709318/

O N JANUARY 27, 2014, the well-known folk singer and left-wing activist Pete Seeger passed away at the age of 94. In his youth, Seeger's radical politics led him to affiliate with the Communist Party of the USA. He joined the Young Communist League in 1936 and the CPUSA itself several years later. After serving in the army during World War II, Seeger resumed his musical career as part of the famous folk act The Weavers. His musical prominence and continued ties to the CPUSA soon brought him to the attention of the House Un-American Activities Committee, which by the early 1950s had adopted the mindset that communism was an alien influence that must be removed root and branch from American society.

On August 18, 1955, Pete Seeger appeared before a session of the House Un-American Activities Committee held in New York City. During his testimony before HUAC, Seeger refused to answer any questions about his political beliefs or associations. He did not, however, invoke the Fifth Amendment to the Constitution as grounds for not answering such questions. Instead, he flatly declined on principle to provide such information. As he told the committee early in his appearance:

I am not going to answer any questions as to my associations, my philosophical or religious beliefs or my political beliefs, or how I voted in any election or any of these private affairs. I think these are very improper questions for any American to be asked, especially under such compulsion as this.

I would be very glad to tell you my life if you want to hear of it. (*Investigation of Communist Activities, New York Area. Part 7, 2449*)

Seeger's refusal to cooperate with HUAC resulted in his being indicted for contempt of Congress. He was ultimately convicted of this charge in March 1961, and sentenced to a year in prison. However, his conviction was overturned on appeal the following year.

Ironically, Seeger had already quietly backed away from the CPUSA by the time he appeared before HUAC. Eventually, he would openly abandon communism, performing at a 1982 benefit for the anti-communist Polish labor union Solidarity and condemning Joseph Stalin in his 1993 memoirs. After being blacklisted in the 1950s, Seeger reemerged in the 1960s as one of the main influences on that decade's folk revival, while his song "We Shall Overcome" became one of the anthems of the civil rights movement. Seeger performed at President Obama's 2009 inauguration and remained active in supporting liberal and left-wing causes until his death.

Primary Sources

Communist Activities Among Youth Groups (Based on Testimony of Harvey M. Matusow). Hearings Before the Committee on Un-American Activities, House of Representatives, Eighty-Second Congress, Second Session. February 6–7, 1952.

Investigation of Communist Activities, New York Area. Part 6: Entertainment. Hearings Before the Committee on Un-American Activities, House of Representatives, Eighty-Fourth Congress, First Session. August 15–16, 1955.

Investigation of Communist Activities, New York Area. Part 7: Entertainment. Hearings Before the Committee on Un-American Activities, House of Representatives, Eighty-Fourth Congress, First Session. August 17–18, 1955.

Testimony of Walter S. Steele Regarding Communist Activities in the U.S. Hearings Before the Committee on Un-American Activities, House of Representatives, Eightieth Congress, First Session. July 21, 1947.

Additional Sources

Lithwick, Dahlia. 'When Pete Seeger Faced Down the House Un-American Activities Committee'. *Slate*, January 28, 2014. http://www.slate.com/blogs /browbeat/2014/01/28/pete_seeger_huac_transcript_full_text_of_anti _communist_hearing_courtesy.html.

Matthews, Dylan. 'The Washington Post picked its top American Communists. Wonkblog begs to differ'. *Washington Post: Wonkblog*, September 26, 2013. https://www.washingtonpost.com/news/wonk/wp/2013/09/26/the -washington-post-picked-its-top-american-communists-wonkblog -begs-to-differ/.

Pareles, Jon. 'Pete Seeger, Champion of Folk Music and Social Change, Dies at 94'. *New York Times*, January 28, 2014. http://www.nytimes.com/2014/01/29/arts /music/pete-seeger-songwriter-and-champion-of-folk-music-dies-at-94.html.

Radosh, Ron. 'Time for Pete Seeger To Repent'. *New York Sun*, June 12, 2007.

Wakin, Daniel J. 'This Just In: Pete Seeger Denounced Stalin Over a Decade Ago'. *New York Times*, September 1, 2007. https://www.nytimes.com/2007/09/01 /arts/music/01seeg.html.

7

Paul Robeson Appears Before HUAC, 1956

Actor/singer Paul Robeson, June 1942. Long controversial for his
outspokenly pro-Soviet views, Robeson would appear before HUAC
on June 12, 1956. In his testimony, he would both passionately
advocate for the rights of African-Americans, while also defending
the Soviet Gulag system of forced labor camps. Source: U.S. Farm
Security Administration/Office of War Information Black & White
Photographs, Library of Congress Prints and Photographs Division:
http://www.loc.gov/pictures/collection/fsa/item/fsa1998023680/PP/

PAUL ROBESON (1898–1976) WAS in many ways a pioneering figure in African-American history. Born in Princeton, New Jersey, Robeson attended Rutgers, where he was a star athlete, among other things becoming a two time Walter Camp All-American in football. He was also a brilliant student. After college, Robeson became a well-known actor and singer. By the 1930s, greatly affected by the pernicious influence of racial discrimination, both on himself and on his people, Robeson became a political activist. By the late 1940s, Robeson had become openly radical and sympathetic to the Soviet Union, which exposed him to much criticism and even persecution. In one infamous incident, a pro-communist concert Robeson gave at Peekskill, New York, in 1949, was met with mob violence. In 1950, in response to his outspoken views, the State Department revoked his American passport, a decision that stood until the Supreme Court ruled it unconstitutional in 1958.

It was the passport issue that would lead Paul Robeson to make his only appearance before the House Un-American Activities Committee. On June 12, 1956, he would testify on the topic of "unauthorized use of United States passports." Robeson would make a stirring defense of his rights as an American citizen, and the civil rights of African-Americans, in remarks addressed to HUAC Chairman Francis Walter (D-PA):

> This is the basis and I am not being tried for whether I am a Communist, I am being tried for fighting for the rights of my people who are still second-class citizens in this UnitedStates of America. My mother was born in your State, Mr. Walter,and my mother was a Quaker, and my ancestors in the time of Washingtonbaked bread for George Washington's troops when they crossedthe Delaware, and my own father was a slave. I stand here strugglingfor the rights of my people to be full citizens in this country and theyare not. They are not in Mississippi and they are not in Montgomery,Ala., and they are not in Washington, and they are nowhere, andthat is why I am here today. You want to shut up every Negro whohas the courage to stand up and fight for the rights of his people, forthe rights of workers and I have been on many a picket line for thesteelworkers too. And that is why I am here today. (*Investigation of the Unauthorized Use*, 4499)

Unfortunately, Robeson's testimony would also feature another prominent aspect of his public advocacy, one that makes him a source of controversy down to the present day: his unstinting support for the Soviet Union and refusal to criticize any aspect of its system or behavior. This, for example, was Robeson's response to HUAC when asked about the USSR's Gulag system of slave labor camps:

> As far as I know about the slave camps, theywere Fascist prisoners who had murdered millions of the Jewishpeople and who would have wiped out millions of the Negro peoplecould they have gotten a hold of them. That is all I know about that. (*Investigation of the Unauthorized Use*, 4506)

Robeson's labeling of the victims of Stalinist oppression as "fascists" was a direct echo of Soviet propaganda, and one rejected by historians. According to scholar Anne Applebaum, whose work *Gulag* is considered close to definitive, some 18 million people passed through Stalin's slave labor camps between 1929–1953, of whom at least 1,000,000 died as a result. (Applebaum, *Gulag*, 580–4)

Justifiably appalled by racism and Jim Crow, and convinced that communism offered a better future for humanity, Robeson was so attracted by the ideals of Soviet communism that he forced himself to overlook its often horrific reality. In the words of his sympathetic left-wing biographer Martin Duberman:

> To the end of his life he would refuse to criticize the Soviets openly, never going further than to make the barest suggestion in private.... that injustice to some individuals must always be expected, however much to be regretted, in an attempt to create a new world dedicated to bettering the lot of the many. (Duberman, *Paul Robeson*, 354)

Today, Paul Robeson is widely regarded as a heroic champion of civil rights. In 2004, he would even be honored by the US Postal Service with his own stamp. In the words of the USPS, "Paul Robeson was a tireless and uncompromising advocate for civil rights and social justice." (USPS, 'African-American on Stamps')

For many eastern Europeans, however, Robeson's unwavering support for the USSR and its actions make him anything but a symbol of freedom. As intellectual historian Ben Alpers put it, "if memories of Robeson have, at least in recent decades, been very positive in the U.S., his legacy is viewed quite differently in the former Soviet bloc." (Alpers, 'Rodriguez, Paul Robeson'). Czech writer Josef Skvorecky famously recounted his feelings about Robeson in his memoir:

In place of [Stan] Kenton, they pushed Paul Robeson at us, and how we hated that black apostle who sang, of his own free will, at open-air concerts in Prague at a time when they were raising the socialist leader Milada Horakova to the gallows...and at a time when great Czech poets (some 10 years later to be "rehabilitated" without exception) were pining away in jails. Well, maybe it was wrong to hold it against Paul Robeson. No doubt he was acting in good faith, convinced that he was fighting for a good cause. But they kept holding him up to us as an exemplary "progressive jazz man," and we hated him. May God rest his-one hopes-innocent soul. (Quoted in Duberman, *Paul Robeson*, 351)

Balancing Paul Robeson's passionate advocacy for civil rights and an end to racial prejudice with his support for Stalinism remains an unavoidable issue when assessing his legacy as a political activist.

Paul Robeson's Testimony Before HUAC

Investigation of the Unauthorized Use of United States Passports, Part 3. Hearings Before the Committee on Un-American Activities, House of Representatives, Eighty-Fourth Congress, Second Session. June 12–13, 1956.

Additional Congressional Testimony by Paul Robeson and his Family

Communist Training Operations: Part 3: Communist Activities and Propaganda Among Youth Groups. Hearings Before the Committee on Un-American Activities, House of Representatives, Eighty Sixth Congress, Second Session. 1960.

Control of Subversive Activities. Hearings before the Committee on the Judiciary, United States Senate, Eightieth Congress, Second Session on H.R. 5852, an act to protect the United States against un-American and subversive activities. 1953.

State Department Information Program — Information Centers, Part 7. Hearing before the Permanent Subcommittee on Investigations of the Committee on Government Operations, United States Senate, Eighty-Third Congress, First Session, pursuant to S. Res. 40, a resolution authorizing the Committee on

Government Operations to employ temporary additional personnel and increasing the amount of expenditures. 1953.

Further Congressional Sources

The American Negro in the Communist Party. Prepared and Released by the Committee on Un-American Activities, U.S. House of Representatives. December 22, 1954.

   Hearings Regarding Communist Infiltration of Minority Groups. Hearings Before the Committee on Un-American Activities, House of Representatives, Eighty First Congress, First Session. 3 pts. 1949–50.

Additional Sources

Alpers, Ben. 'Rodriguez, Paul Robeson, and Complicated Narratives of Reception.' *U.S. Intellectual History Blog*, April 8, 2013. https://s-usih .org/2013/04/rodriguez-paul-robeson-and-complicated-narratives-of -reception/

Applebaum, Anne. *Gulag: A History.* New York: Doubleday, 2003.

Duberman, Martin Bauml. *Paul Robeson.* New York: Knopf, 1988.

National Archives and Records Administration. "The Many Faces of Paul Robeson." https://www.archives.gov/education/lessons/robeson.

United States Postal Service. 'African-Americans on Stamps: A Celebration of African-American Heritage.' *USPS Publication No. 354*, January 2004. https://about.usps.com/publications/pub354/welcome.htm.

8

"A Travesty Upon the Word 'Investigation'"

Mary Knowles and the Plymouth Meeting Controversy

B Y 1956, THE COMMUNIST Party of the United States of America had ceased to be relevant. Having barely survived the intensive internal security measures implemented by the U.S. government in the early 1950s, the main blow to the CPUSA came, ironically enough, from the party's Soviet patron. Nikita Khrushchev's February 1956 "secret speech," which implicated his predecessor Joseph Stalin in numerous crimes, brutally disabused many party members of their notion that Stalin's Soviet Union represented a bright pinnacle of human progress. Most CPUSA members left the party by the end of the decade.

The demise of the CPUSA did not, however, stop the House Un-American Activities Committee from continuing its relentless campaign to root out any vestige of communist influence from American society, however trivial. By the mid-1950s, the committee's public hearings into the remnants of the CPUSA had evolved into a performative shaming ritual in which those witnesses who took the Fifth Amendment to avoid self-incrimination were then subject to a variety of social sanctions, frequently including denial of employment.

In the summer of 1956, HUAC would travel to Philadelphia to hold a hearing into a Quaker-run local library that employed a librarian who once had CPUSA ties. On this occasion, however, the library and librarian in question defied HUAC and the culture of performative shaming it represented.

Mary Knowles and the William Jeanes Memorial Library

In August 1953, the William Jeanes Memorial Library, in Plymouth Meeting, PA, found itself in need of a replacement librarian after the current librarian broke her leg. The library, run by the local Quaker community, hired Mary Knowles, a librarian who had recently moved to the area from Boston. After the previous librarian decided to retire, Knowles was hired as the new permanent librarian in September 1954.

Knowles was praised for her excellent work at Jeanes Memorial, but she had one drawback: she was very much a target of the congressional countersubversive apparatus represented by HUAC and several other committees. Mary's former husband, Clyde Knowles, was a CPUSA activist, and from 1945–47, she worked as secretary at the CPUSA-affiliated Samuel Adams School in Boston. In May 1953, a former Boston-area CPUSA member named Herbert Philbrick identified Mary Knowles as "a member of the Communist Party, and in fact a member of my own pro-group underground cell" in testimony before the Senate Internal Security Subcommittee (SISS). (*Subversive Influence*, Part 9, 944)

Philbrick's certainty in identifying Knowles as a communist before SISS stood in stark contrast to his closed-door testimony before HUAC in 1951. At this earlier appearance, Philbrick had answered "Not that I recall at this time" when asked if Mary Knowles was a CPUSA member. (*Expose of Communist Activities*, 131) Nevertheless, Philbrick's improved memory resulted in Knowles being fired from her job at the South Norwood (MA) Branch Library, and herself being called to testify before SISS on May 21, 1953, where she invoked the Fifth Amendment. Ironically, it was SISS's pursuit of Knowles that made her available to take the Plymouth Meeting job.

Knowles was upfront with the Plymouth Meeting Library Committee about her issues. The committee and its chair, Lillian Tapley, decided to employ her regardless. Upon Knowles's permanent employment in September 1954, controversy ensued. The local township withdrew its financial support from the library, and the school board instructed students not to use Jeanes Library. By early 1955, the clamor had grown more intense, as groups such as the American Legion and Daughters of the American Revolution called for Knowles to be fired. The library committee, however, despite several resignations, remained firmly on Knowles's side.

Enter the Fund for the Republic

In the midst of this controversy, there were two events that further exacerbated the situation. First, in May 1955, a civil liberties nonprofit called the

SENATE CALLS MRS. KNOWLES FOR HEARING

7/29/55

Plymouth Librarian Summoned by Internal Security Sub-Committee

Headline from the Norristown (PA) Times-Herald, July 1955. Image via Historical Society of Montgomery County. Source: https://hsmcpa.org/ index.php/component/k2/item/16– the-plymouth-meeting-controversy

Fund for the Republic granted Plymouth Meeting a $5,000 award "in recognition of its forthright stand in defense of individual freedom" by employing Mary Knowles. The Fund's president, former University of Chicago head Robert Maynard Hutchins, expressed the hope "that Plymouth Monthly Meeting's example will be followed elsewhere in America, particularly when our libraries—which seem to be a special target of self-appointed censors and amateur loyalty experts—are involved." (Quoted in Mayer, *Robert Maynard Hutchins*, 432)

The Fund's award only served to enrage the countersubversives, in Congress and elsewhere, who wanted Knowles fired. This led to the second event, which was that Mary Knowles was again subpoenaed to testify before SISS. Testifying on September 15, 1955, she once again declined to cooperate with the committee. This time, however, she did so without invoking the Fifth Amendment, but rather by making the following argument:

> First, that I am not a Communist; that I am not a member of the Communist Party, and that for many, many years I have had no connection, direct or indirect, with any organization on the Attorney General's list.

Further than that I have no knowledge of any matters concerning national security; I have no knowledge of any matters concerning the Internal Security Act of 1950; I have no knowledge of any matters of subversion, sabotage, or espionage, of infiltration, of violent overthrow of the Government, of any acts concerning any foreign powers or any other illegal act.

In view of these things and the fact that I am a private citizen employed in a private institution under the care of a religious organization, I feel that I have no information that would be within the power or the jurisdiction of this duly organized committee to ask of me. (*Subversive Influence*, Part 14, 549)

As a result of her refusal to cooperate with SISS, the Senate voted on April 17, 1956 to hold Mary Knowles in contempt of Congress.

HUAC Enters the Picture

In addition to supporting Plymouth Meeting for retaining Mary Knowles, the Fund for the Republic with much fanfare also produced a report critical of blacklisting in the entertainment industry, which was published in late June 1956. This drew the ire of the House Un-American Activities Committee and its chair, Rep. Francis Walter (D-PA). In May 1956, HUAC quietly began an investigation of the Fund, publicly announcing its investigation in June.

After holding six days of hearings in early July criticizing the Fund's report on blacklisting, Walter took advantage of a subcommittee visit to Philadelphia in mid-July to hold a one-day hearing on the Plymouth Meeting controversy. Held on July 18, 1956, the hearing was officially about the Fund's award to Plymouth Meeting. It soon became clear, however, that the hearing was little more than an attempt to shame and embarrass both Plymouth Meeting and the Fund for the Republic. Of the six witnesses called, four were local residents critical of Mary Knowles's employment. A fifth was Maureen Black Ogden, an investigator for the Fund who recommended the Plymouth Meeting award. She was of course harshly grilled by Walter's subcommittee. Only Lillian Tapley was allowed to make the case on behalf of the Plymouth Meeting Library Committee.

Representative Francis Walter (D-PA),
Chair of HUAC from 1955–63. Walter was
instrumental in inserting HUAC into the
Plymouth Meeting controversy. Image via
Biographical Directory of the United States
Congress. Source: https://bioguide.congress.
gov/search/bio/W000108

The outrageous nature of the hearing was aptly summarized in a July
24 letter written by nine Philadelphia area Quakers, and addressed to the
HUAC members not present at the hearing:

It is our opinion that what took place was a travesty upon the word
"investigation" and a mockery of the idea of inquiry. It appears rather
to have been an organized attempt to present selected facts in the light
most discreditable to the Fund for the Republic, Inc. We refer in part to
the number and order in which witnesses were called; the close questioning of witnesses of one point of view, and the obvious sympathy with
those of another; the repeated rejection of proffers of fact by individual

witnesses; the deliberate cultivation of hearsay testimony which fitted their thesis; and like irregularities. (Quoted in The *Plymouth Meeting Controversy*, 30)

Postscript

In January 1957, Mary Knowles was convicted of contempt of Congress for her September 1955 testimony before SISS. Her conviction would be overturned by the Supreme Court in 1961. The Plymouth Meeting Library Committee remained steadfast in its support of Mary Knowles until the controversy subsided, and Jeanes Library thrived under her leadership. Knowles remained at William Jeanes Memorial Library until her retirement in 1979.

Perhaps the final word on the Plymouth Meeting controversy belongs to Hutchins biographer Milton Mayer, in describing Mary Knowles:

Mrs. Mary Knowles did not appear to be redoubtable, but she was; more redoubtable, in the end, than the United States Congress, the Federal Bureau of Investigation, the American Legion, and the most redoubtable representatives of the American press. (Mayer, *Robert Maynard Hutchins*, 430)

Primary Sources Featuring Testimony by Mary Knowles

Subversive Influence in the Educational Process, Part 10: Hearings Before the Subcommittee to Investigate the Administration of the Internal Security Act and Other Internal Security Laws of the Committee on the Judiciary, United States Senate, Eighty-Third Congress, First Session. 1953.

Subversive Influence in the Educational Process, Part 14: Hearing Before the Subcommittee to Investigate the Administration of the Internal Security Act and Other Internal Security Laws of the Committee on the Judiciary, United States Senate, Eighty-Fourth Congress, First Session. 1955.

Sources Featuring Testimony Referring to Mary Knowles

Investigation of the Award by the Fund for the Republic, Inc., Plymouth Meeting, PA. Hearing before the Committee on Un-American Activities, House of Representatives, Eighty-Fourth Congress, Second Session. 1956.

Investigation of Un-American Propaganda Activities in the U.S. Appendix, Part 9: Communist Front Organizations: First Section. Special Committee on Un-American Activities, House of Representatives, Seventy-Eighth Congress, Second Session. 1944.

Subversive Influence in the Educational Process, Part 9: Hearings Before the Subcommittee to Investigate the Administration of the Internal Security Act and Other Internal Security Laws of the Committee on the Judiciary, United States Senate, Eighty-Third Congress, First Session. 1953.

Testimony of Walter S. Steele Regarding Communist Activities in the United States. Hearings before the Committee on Un-American Activities, House of Representatives, Eightieth Congress, First Session. 1947.

U.S. House. Committee on Un-American Activities. *Expose of Communist Activities in the State of Massachusetts.* (HRG-1951–UAH-0036; Date: Jun. 18–21, 1951). Text in: ProQuest® Unpublished Hearings Digital Collection.

Additional Sources

Goodman, Walter. *The Committee: The Extraordinary Career of the House Committee on Un-American Activities.* New York: Farrar, Straus, and Giroux, 1968.

Hepler, Allison. *McCarthyism in the Suburbs: Quakers, Communists, and the Children's Librarian.* Lanham, MD: Lexington Books, 2018.

Jenkins, Philip. *The Cold War at Home: The Red Scare in Pennsylvania, 1945–1960.* Chapel Hill: University of North Carolina Press, 1999.

Mayer, Milton. *Robert Maynard Hutchins: A Memoir.* Berkeley: University of California Press, c1993 1993. http://ark.cdlib.org/ark:/13030/ft4w10061d/.

The Plymouth Meeting Controversy: A Report Prepared for the Civil Liberties Committee of the Philadelphia Yearly Meeting of the Religious Society of Friends. 1957. https://babel.hathitrust.org/cgi/pt?id=mdp.39015031054029 &view=1up&seq=5&skin=2021.

Reeves, Thomas C. *Freedom and the Foundation: The Fund for the Republic in the Era of McCarthyism.* New York: Knopf, 1969.

Sullivan, Nancy. "The Plymouth Meeting Controversy." *Historical Society of Montgomery County (blog),* March 9, 2017. https://hsmcpa.org/index.php /component/k2/item/16–the-plymouth-meeting-controversy.

PART THREE

The Decline of Countersubversion

1960–77

The First NSA Defection

1960

NSA defectors William H. Martin and Bernon F. Mitchell at the Moscow press conference announcing their defection, July 1, 1960. Image via National Security Agency Cryptologic Heritage website and Internet Archive: https://web .archive.org/web/20150918045935/https://www.nsa.gov/about /cryptologic_heritage/60th/interactive_timeline/Content/1960s/full_images /MartinandMitchell.jpg

I T'S A STORY FILLED with uncanny parallels that could be plucked directly from this century's headlines: young men working with the National Security Agency (NSA) who grow disillusioned by what they find, abscond with classified information, and end up seeking asylum in

Moscow. Fifty-three years before Edward Snowden left his job as a consultant with the NSA and ultimately pursued refuge in Moscow, a pair of disillusioned NSA employees, William H. Martin and Bernon F. Mitchell, defected to the Soviet Union.

Martin and Mitchell started with the NSA in 1957. According to subsequent government investigations, both may have secretly joined the Communist Party and likely visited Cuba in late 1959. According to authors Christopher Andrew and Vasili Mitrokhin, Mitchell visited the Soviet embassy in Mexico City in December 1959 and asked for political asylum. Despite KGB efforts to persuade him to stay in NSA and serve as an agent, he and Martin insisted that they preferred to defect. On June 25, 1960, Martin and Mitchell boarded a flight from Washington for Mexico City. From there, they traveled subsequently to Cuba and then the Soviet Union. On August 1, the Department of Defense announced that Martin and Mitchell were missing, later acknowledging on August 5 that it was likely that the two men had fled to the Eastern Bloc. On August 11, 1960, William H. Martin and Bernon F. Mitchell were officially granted asylum in the USSR and each awarded a monthly allowance of 500 rubles, roughly equal to their NSA salaries.

On September 6, 1960, Martin and Mitchell held a press conference in Moscow to announce their defections. Martin explained their decision as follows:

> We were employees of the highly secret National Security Agency, which gathers communications intelligence from almost all nations of the world for use by the U.S. Government. However, the simple act that the U.S. Government is engaged in delving into the secrets of other nations had little or nothing to do with our decision to defect. Our main dissatisfaction concerns some of the practices the United States uses in gathering intelligence information. We were worried about the U.S. policy of deliberately violating the airspace of other nations and the U.S. Government's practice of lying about such violations in a manner intended to mislead public opinion. Furthermore, we were disenchanted by the U.S. Government's practice of intercepting and deciphering the secret communications of its own allies. Finally, we objected to the

fact that the U.S. Government was willing to go so far as to recruit agents from among the personnel of its allies. ("NSA/CSS 60th Anniversary Timeline")

The very next day, September 7, 1960, the House Un-American Activities Committee would launch an investigation of the Martin-Mitchell defections and their potential impact on American national security. HUAC's investigation would last 13 months, using over 2,000 hours of staff work and producing 16 executive-session (closed to the public) hearings, featuring testimony from 34 current or former NSA employees.

In August 1962, HUAC would release a 23 page report summarizing its findings. Among other things, the report would question the validity of the polygraph as a tool for detecting possible security risks. In a reflection of then prevailing attitudes toward homosexuality, the document also made much of allegations that Martin and Mitchell were gay, citing this as a factor in their defection. Journalist Rick Anderson, however, has shown that Martin and Mitchell were not, in fact, gay.

An NSA historical overview of the case noted that "It is believed that there was very little damage" done to U.S. intelligence efforts as a result of the defection. ("Betrayers of the Trust") This is confirmed by Andrew and Mitrokhin, who write that the KGB was "disappointed" in the quality of the information supplied by Martin and Mitchell. (Andrew & Mitrokhin, *The Sword and the Shield*, 179) The feeling was soon to be mutual. Despite their relatively generous stipends and both marrying Soviet women, Martin and Mitchell quickly became disillusioned by the realities of life in the USSR. Neither man ever returned to the United States: Martin dying in Mexico in 1987 and Mitchell in Russia in 2001.

Primary Sources

National Security Agency. "NSA/CSS 60th Anniversary Timeline – 1960s." https://www.nsa.gov/Helpful-Links/NSA-FOIA/Declassification -Transparency-Initiatives/Historical-Releases/NSA-60th-Timeline /smdpage14701/20/.

Security Practices in the National Security Agency (Defection of Bernon F. Mitchell and William H. Martin). Report by the Committee on Un-American Activities,

House of Representatives, Eighty-Seventh Congress, Second Session. August 13, 1962.

Additional Sources

Anderson, Rick. 'Before Edward Snowden: "Sexual deviates" and the NSA'. *Salon*, July 1, 2013. https://www.salon.com/2013/07/01/before_edward_snowden _sexual_deviates_and_the_nsa/.

Andrew, Christopher and Vasili Mitrokhin. *The Sword and the Shield: The Mitrokhin Archive and the Secret History of the KGB.* New York: Basic Books, 1999.

"Betrayers of the Trust." *National Security Agency Cryptologic Almanac*, May-June 2002. (Available via Internet Archive) https://archive.org/details /Betrayers_of_the_Trust-nsa.

2

Fred Hampton and the Black Panthers

THE FILM *Judas and the Black Messiah* depicts the life and death of Fred Hampton, a leader of the Chicago branch of the Black Panther Party (BPP). Hampton was killed on December 4, 1969, in a raid by Chicago police officers on the apartment where he was staying with eight other members of the BPP. At the time, the Chicago Police Department and the Illinois State's Attorney's Office claimed the police shootings of Hampton and another Panther killed during the raid were acts of justified self-defense. Subsequent investigation made it abundantly clear that these explanations were false.

The Black Panther Party

The Black Panther Party for Self-Defense was founded in Oakland, CA, in late 1966, and soon spread to a number of urban areas with large African-American populations. From its beginnings the BPP saw itself as a revolutionary movement that embraced Maoism and, if necessary, armed resistance to local, state, and federal authorities. They regarded racism as endemic to the American socio-political system, and believed that only a total rejection of that system could free African-Americans from its effects. The various BPP chapters stockpiled weapons, often confronted police while armed, and cultivated a militant, paramilitary culture in their ranks. The movement's rhetoric was often violent, and glorified if not incited anti-police violence.

The BPP's militantly anti-police posture was very much a response to the all-too widespread police violence against African-American communities. Not simply acts of police brutality and even killing, but also daily acts

Members of the BPP in front of the Washington state capitol in
Olympia, WA, February 28, 1969. Source: Seattle Black Panther
Party History and Memory Project: http://depts.washington.
edu/civilr/uploads/2-28-69%20cr2.jpg

of harassment and petty humiliation. Coupled with the widespread urban
unrest of the 1960s, and rising overall crime rates, tensions between many
urban police departments and African-American communities reached the
breaking point. As a 1973 independent report on the killing of Fred Hampton described it, there was now an "atmosphere of anger, fear, and mutual
hostility...between black Chicagoans and the police." The report continued:

> That such an atmosphere existed could come as no surprise to
> anyone even casually familiar with the state of police-community
> relations in black areas of American cities at that time. Chicago's
> experience during the late 1960s may have been especially violent and
> tense, but it was fundamentally no different from the situation that

prevailed in almost every major urban center in the country. (Wilkins and Clark, *Search and Destroy*, 28)

Through their often violent words, and occasional actions, the BPP both reflected this dynamic and contributed to it. Their radical ideology and rhetoric soon made them a major target of local, state, and federal law enforcement agencies. FBI Director J. Edgar Hoover described the BPP as "without question...the greatest threat to the internal security of the country [among] violence-prone black-extremist groups." (Quoted in Wilkins and Clark, *Search and Destroy*, 11)

At Hoover's direction, the Panthers soon became one of the top targets of the FBI's controversial Counter Intelligence Program (COINTELPRO). Initiated in 1956, expanded starting in 1965, and continued until 1971, COINTELPRO was designed not simply to monitor groups suspected of seeking the violent overthrow of the U.S. government, but sought to actively disrupt and sabotage their operations, through the use of informants and disinformation. The BPP branch in Chicago, established in 1968, soon became a major COINTELPRO focus.

The Killing of Fred Hampton

Fred Hampton, eloquent and charismatic, soon emerged as the leader of the BPP in Chicago. While using rhetoric typical of the Panther movement, most of his activities involved non-violent organizing and community outreach efforts. Over the course of 1969, however, a number of violent incidents between Panthers and Chicago police took place, often instigated by the latter. According to a May 1970 federal grand jury report, as a result of these incidents "two police and one Panther were killed; fourteen police and four Panthers were wounded or injured; and there had been over sixty arrests of Panthers for violations ranging from attempted murder and kidnapping to minor traffic violations." (United States District Court, *Report*, 12)

The evidence makes clear that, by the time of the December 4th raid, Chicago police saw themselves as at war with the BPP. The raid itself was prompted in part by information provided by the FBI, and facilitated by an FBI informant. Of the nine individuals in the apartment at 2337 W. Monroe Street, Hampton and another Panther, Mark Clark, were killed, and four others were wounded. Two policemen suffered light injuries. The police and state's attorney insisted that the deaths and injuries were the result of the officers being met with armed resistance while trying to serve a lawful warrant. All seven survivors were charged, with a total of 31 criminal counts between them.

The immediate aftermath of the raid sparked a huge outcry, especially among the African-American community. An estimated 5,000 mourners came to Fred Hampton's funeral. Almost immediately, the Panthers questioned the official version of events. Evidence soon bore out their complaints. An FBI forensics analysis showed that only one shot was fired by the Panthers at 2337 W. Monroe. By contrast, the police fired as many as 99 rounds. This clearly refuted the claims of a shootout, and the charges against the survivors were soon dismissed. Hampton, who was unconscious and possibly drugged during the raid, was shot four times while lying in bed.

The independent 1973 investigation concluded that:

> Every indication is that the raid, contrary to its stated objectives, was conceived and planned as an armed confrontation with leaders of the Illinois chapter of the Black Panther Party under circumstances in which the planners of the raid knew-or should have known-that loss of life was almost inevitable. (Wilkins and Clark, *Search and Destroy*, 237–8)

The killing of Fred Hampton and the federal/state law enforcement campaign against the BPP reflect a number of strands of American history, including racism, police brutality, and the often violent tumult America experienced during the late 1960s. It also marked perhaps the culmination of the 20th Century countersubversive mindset that saw almost any form of social protest as simply the product of radical subversion, to be suppressed by extralegal and even unconstitutional means if necessary. As civil rights leader Reverend Ralph Abernathy stated at Fred Hampton's funeral:

> If they can do this to the Black Panthers today, who will they do it to tomorrow? If they succeed in repressing the Black Panthers, it won't be long
> before they crush any party in sight-maybe your party, maybe my party. (Quoted in Wilkins and Clark, *Search and Destroy*, 5)

Primary Sources

Black Panther Party. Hearings Before the Committee on Internal Security, House of Representatives, Ninety-First Congress, Second Session. 1970–71, 4 pts.

The Black Panther Party: Its Origin and Development as Reflected in its Official Weekly Newspaper The Black Panther, Black Community News Service: Staff Study. Committee on Internal Security, House of Representatives, Ninety-First Congress, Second Session. 1970.

Domestic Intelligence Operations for Internal Security Purposes: Part 1: Hearings Before the Committee on Internal Security, House of Representatives, Ninety-Third Congress, Second Session. 1974.

Extent of Subversion in the New Left, Part 4: Testimony of Charles Siragusa and Ronald L. Brooks: Hearings Before the Subcommittee to Investigate the Administration of the Internal Security Act and Other Internal Security Laws of the Committee on the Judiciary, United States Senate, Ninety-First Congress, Second Session. June 10, 1970.

Gun-Barrel Politics, the Black Panther Party, 1966–1971. Report by the Committee on Internal Security, House of Representatives, Ninety-Second Congress, First Session. August 18, 1971.

Riots, Civil and Criminal Disorders, Part 20: Hearings before the United States Senate Committee on Government Operations, Permanent Subcommittee on Investigations, Ninety-First Congress, First Session. 1969.

Riots, Civil and Criminal Disorders, Part 25: Hearings before the United States Senate Committee on Government Operations, Permanent Subcommittee on Investigations, Ninety-First Congress, Second Session. 1970.

United States District Court, Northern District of Illinois, Eastern Division. *Report of the January 1970 Grand Jury.* Washington, D.C.: U.S. Government Printing Office, 1970. (Available via Internet Archive) https://archive.org /details/Grand-Jury-Fred-Hampton-1970.

Further Federal Government Sources

Intelligence Activities Senate Resolution 21: Vol. 6: Federal Bureau of Investigation. Hearings before the Select Committee to Study Governmental Operations with Respect to Intelligence Activities, United States Senate, Ninety-Fourth Congress, First Session. 1975.

National Archives and Records Administration. "African American Heritage: Fred Hampton (August 30, 1948 – December 4, 1969)." https://www .archives.gov/research/african-americans/individuals/fred-hampton.

National Archives and Records Administration. "Rediscovering Black History: Fred Hampton: Vanguard Revolutionary." December 4, 2019. https:// rediscovering-black-history.blogs.archives.gov/2019/12/04/fred -hampton-vanguard-revolutionary/.

Additional Sources

Austin, Curtis J. *Up Against the Wall: Violence in the Making and Unmaking of the Black Panther Party*. Fayetteville: University of Arkansas Press, 2006.

The Black Panthers Speak. ed. Philip S. Foner. Chicago: Haymarket Books, 2014.

Blackstock, Nelson. *Cointelpro: The FBI's Secret War on Political Freedom*. New York: Vintage Books, 1976.

Haas, Jeffrey. *The Assassination of Fred Hampton: How the FBI and the Chicago Police Murdered a Black Panther*. Chicago: Lawrence Hill Books/Chicago Review Press, 2009.

Seattle Civil Rights & Labor History Project. "Seattle Black Panther Party History and Memory Project." University of Washington. http://depts .washington.edu/civilr/BPP.htm.

Taylor, Flint. *The Torture Machine: Racism and Police Violence in Chicago*. Chicago: Haymarket Books, 2019.

Wilkins, Roy and Ramsey Clark. *Search And Destroy: A Report by the Commission of Inquiry into the Black Panthers and the Police*. New York: Metropolitan Applied Research Center, 1973. (Available via Internet Archive) https://archive.org/details/Search-And-Destroy-1973/.

Williams, Jakobi. *From the Bullet to the Ballot: The Illinois Chapter of the Black Panther Party and Racial Coalition Politics in Chicago*. Chapel Hill: University of North Carolina Press, 2013.

PART FOUR

Espionage, Disinformation and Political Warfare in the Cold War

Active Measures

❧

ATERM USED TO REFER to Soviet efforts to influence and manipulate
public opinion in other countries during the Cold War, Active Measures has gained a newfound currency in light of the 2016 election
influence campaign by Russian intelligence, as well as their overall attempts
to shape popular opinion and discourse in the social media environment.
This post seeks to put current Russian active measures efforts into a broader
historical context.

What are Active Measures?

"Our friends in Moscow call it 'dezinformatsiya.' Our enemies in
America call it 'active measures,' and I, dear friends, call it 'my favorite
pastime.'"
　　—Col. Rolf Wagenbreth, Director of Department X, East German
foreign intelligence (STASI) (Quoted in Schoen and Lamb, *Deception,
Disinformation, and Strategic Communications*, 8)

According to the authors of a 2017 study, "The term "Active Measures' came
into use in the USSR in the 1950s to describe overt and covert techniques for
influencing events and behaviour in foreign countries. Disinformation – the
intentional dissemination of false information – is just one of many elements
that made up active measures operations." (Cull, et al., *Soviet Subversion,
Disinformation and Propaganda*, 6) Other techniques included circulating
forged documents, false or misleading news stories ("fake news"), and using
agents of influence to shape both public opinion and policymaking.

Cartoon published in Pravda, October
31, 1986, alleging that AIDS was the
work of American biological warfare
researchers. Reproduced in: Geissler,
Erhard and Robert Hunt Sprinkle.
"Disinformation Squared: Was the HIV-
from-Fort-Detrick Myth a Stasi Success?"
Politics and the Life Sciences: The
Journal of the Association for Politics
and the Life Sciences 32 2 (2013): 2–99.
P.27. DOI:10.2990/32_2_2

The Height of Active Measures

During the Cold War, Soviet active measures reached their height during
the 1970s and early 1980s. Numerous forgeries and fake news stories were
disseminated to influence foreign governments and populations against the
United States. Examples include a forged US military document implying
American desire to use nuclear weapons on European soil in the event of war;
and a forged letter, purportedly from the US Naval Attaché in Rome, meant
to lend credence to a KGB disinformation story that the US was storing chemical and bacteriological weapons at a base in Naples, Italy.

Most famously, a disinformation campaign begun in 1983 and intensified in 1985 claimed that the AIDS virus had been created in a US biological warfare research facility. Dubbed Operation Denver, the campaign incorporated the efforts of the KGB's Service A, responsible for active measures efforts, along with their counterparts in the East German Stasi, and other Warsaw Pact secret services.

In a September 7, 1985 message to the Bulgarian intelligence service, the KGB stated that:

> We are conducting a series of [active] measures in connection with the appearance in recent years in the USA of a new and dangerous disease, "Acquired Immune Deficiency Syndrome – AIDS" ..., and its subsequent, large-scale spread to other countries, including those in Western Europe. The goal of these measures is to create a favorable opinion for us abroad that this disease is the result of secret experiments with a new type of biological weapon by the secret services of the USA and the Pentagon that spun out of control. (quoted in Selvage and Nehring, 'Operation "Denver"')

Beginning in 1981, the US government began aggressively pushing back against Soviet active measures efforts, bringing to light and debunking numerous Soviet forgeries and disinformation stories. A special interagency Active Measures Working Group, relying heavily on the State Department and the US Information Agency, was formed for this purpose. It released its first publication, *Forgery, Disinformation, Political Operations: Soviet Active Measures*, in October 1981. By 1986–87, rebutting the AIDS campaign became a special focus for this body. The Soviets began to back away from the AIDS active measures campaign by late 1987, without abandoning it entirely. They also launched new active measures efforts, such as allegations that Latin American children were being abducted and having their organs harvested for the benefit of wealthy Americans in need of an organ transplant.

The Return of Active Measures

With the end of the Cold War, the concept of active measures seemed to be merely a footnote to history. Under pressure from the United States, the post-Soviet Russian intelligence services abandoned the term "active measures". However, they remained committed to the general concept, and simply re-dubbed it "support measures." (Juurvee, *The Resurrection of "Active Measures"*, 3)

With Vladimir Putin's return to the Russian presidency in 2012, and the subsequent deterioration of relations between Russia and the West, active measures have reemerged as a key part of the Kremlin's foreign policy. In particular, the Russian efforts to influence the 2016 American presidential election shows post-Soviet Russia's continued commitment to active measures, as well as its adaptation of them to the digital age.

As documented in Special Counsel Robert Mueller's March 2019 report on Russian interference in the 2016 election, the Russians pursued a two-track approach. On the first track, Russia's military intelligence service, the GRU, began hacking into email accounts of individuals and organizations affiliated with the Democratic Party and Hillary Clinton campaign in March 2016. In July of that year, they used an online cutout to begin sharing the hacked emails with WikiLeaks, who began publishing them later that month. The hacked emails released through WikiLeaks, were, in Mueller's words, "designed and timed to interfere with the 2016 U.S. presidential election and undermine the Clinton Campaign." (Mueller, *Report on the Investigation*, 36)

The second track once more involved the spreading of disinformation and "fake news", in this case through social media via troll and bot accounts. This social media active measures campaign was not conducted directly by the Russian government, but through a private organization called the Internet Research Agency (IRA). Funded by Yevgeniy Prigozhin, a Russian oligarch with close ties to Putin, "The IRA conducted social media operations targeted at large U.S. audiences with the goal of sowing discord in the U.S. political system." (Mueller, Report on the Investigation, 14) The IRA's widespread use of fake accounts on Facebook, Twitter, and Instagram soon saw it dubbed the "troll farm". As with the GRU's efforts, the IRA campaign "favored presidential candidate Donald J. Trump and disparaged presidential candidate Hillary Clinton." (Mueller, *Report on the Investigation*, 1)

The Russian campaign to interfere in the 2016 U.S. presidential election shows beyond doubt that active measures have returned with a vengeance.

Primary Sources

Forgery, Disinformation, Political Operations: Soviet Active Measures. U.S. Department of State, Bureau of Public Affairs, Office of Public Communication, Editorial Division, 1981.

Howard, Philip N., Bharath Ganesh, Dimitra Liotsiou, John Kelly & Camille François. "The IRA, Social Media and Political Polarization in the United States, 2012–2018." Working Paper 2018.2. Oxford, UK: Project on Computational Propaganda. https://demtech.oii.ox.ac.uk/wp-content /uploads/sites/12/2018/12/The-IRA-Social-Media-and-Political-Polarization .pdf.

Mueller, Robert S, III. *Report on the Investigation into Russian Interference in the 2016 Presidential Election: Submitted Pursuant to 28 C.F.R. '600.8(c).* Washington, D.C.: U.S. Government Publishing Office, 2019. https://purl .fdlp.gov/GPO/gpo119314.

Soviet Active Measures: An Update. U.S. Department of State, Bureau of Public Affairs, Office of Public Communication, Editorial Division, 1982.

Soviet Active Measures: Hearings Before the Permanent Select Committee on Intelligence, House of Representatives, Ninety-Seventh Congress, Second Session, 1982.

Soviet Active Measures: September 1983. U.S. Department of State, Bureau of Public Affairs, Office of Public Communication, Editorial Division, 1983.

Soviet Covert Action (The Forgery Offensive): Hearings Before the Subcommittee on Oversight of the Permanent Select Committee on Intelligence, House of Representatives, Ninety-Sixth Congress, Second Session. 1980.

Soviet Influence Activities: A Report on Active Measures and Propaganda, 1986–87. U.S. Department of State, 1987.

Soviet Influence Activities: A Report on Active Measures and Propaganda, 1987–1988. U.S. Department of State, 1989.

The U.S.S.R.'s AIDS Disinformation Campaign. U.S. Department of State, 1987.

Additional Sources

Boghardt, Thomas. "Operation INFEKTION: Soviet Bloc Intelligence and Its AIDS Disinformation Campaign." *Studies in Intelligence* 53 (4), December 2009. https://www.iwp.edu/wp-content/uploads/2019/05/20140905 _BoghardtAIDSMadeintheUSA.pdf.

Cull, Nicholas J., Vasily Gatov, Peter Pomerantsev, Anne Applebaum and Alistair Shawcross. *Soviet Subversion, Disinformation and Propaganda: How the West Fought Against it. An Analytic History, with Lessons for the Present: Final Report.* LSE Consulting, October 2017. https://www.lse.ac.uk/iga/assets /documents/arena/2018/Jigsaw-Soviet-Subversion-Disinformation-and -Propaganda-Final-Report.pdf.

Jones, Seth G. Russian *Meddling in the United States: The Historical Context of the Mueller Report. CSIS Briefs,* Center for Strategic & International

Studies, March 27, 2019. https://www.csis.org/analysis
/russian-meddling-united-states-historical-context-mueller-report.

Juurvee, Ivo. *Hybrid CoE Strategic Analysis 7: The resurrection of 'active measures':
Intelligence services as a part of Russia's influencing toolbox.* Hybrid CoE, May 2,
2018. https://www.hybridcoe.fi/publications/hybrid-coe-strategic
-analysis-7–the-resurrection-of-active-measures-intelligence-services
-as-a-part-of-russias-influencing-toolbox/.

Schoen, Fletcher and Christopher J. Lamb. *Deception, Disinformation, and
Strategic Communications: How One Interagency Group Made a Major
Difference.* Washington, D.C.: National Defense University Press, 2012.
http://purl.fdlp.gov/GPO/gpo60199.

Selvage, Douglas and Christopher Nehring. 'Operation "Denver": KGB and Stasi
Disinformation regarding AIDS.' *Sources and Methods Blog*, Woodrow Wilson
Center, July 22, 2019. https://www.wilsoncenter.org/blog-post
/operation-denver-kgb-and-stasi-disinformation-regarding-aids.

The "Neighbors"

The GRU in America, from "Ales" to "Fancy Bear"

Official emblem of the GRU. Courtesy of
Wikipedia: https://en.wikipedia.org/wiki
/File:Emblem_of_the_GRU.svg

W HEN MOST AMERICANS THINK of Soviet/Russian intelligence activity in our country, they primarily think of the state security services, the KGB (Committee for State Security) and its main post-Soviet successor, the FSB (Federal Security Service). Some of the most famous and effective Soviet/Russian intelligence operations in the United States, however, have involved an organization few Americans have heard of, one dubbed "the neighbors" by their KGB/FSB rivals: the Glavnoye Razvedyvatel'noye Upravlenie (GRU), the Main Intelligence Directorate of the Armed Forces General Staff: Soviet/Russian military intelligence. From the recruitment of State Department official Alger Hiss in the 1930s, to the Cuban Missile Crisis, to the 2016 election-related hacking of the Democratic National Committee (DNC), the GRU has played an important yet over-looked role in many of Moscow's most influential intelligence activities in this country.

The GRU: Introduction and Overview

The first iteration of Soviet military intelligence was founded in November 1918, but it was not until April 1921 that the body which would become the GRU was formed. Known as the Razvedupr, short for intelligence directorate, or the Fourth Directorate, it was not officially called the GRU until February 16, 1942, a name it carried through most of its history. In 2010, its name was officially shortened to Main Directorate, or GU. However, it is still commonly referred to as the GRU, and this name will be used in the rest of this essay.

Tasked with primarily gathering military-related intelligence, the GRU has often defined this in the broadest sense, gathering political, strategic, economic, and technological information. In addition to running networks of agents, GRU also controls military and naval attaches at Russian embassies, and has extensive paramilitary capabilities.

Throughout its history, the GRU has had a complicated relationship with the political security services, the KGB and its post-Soviet successors, the FSB and the SVR (Foreign Intelligence Service.) On the one hand, as a part of the military, it has no direct organizational ties to the other security services. In fact, there has often been a highly intense, competitive, rivalry between the GRU and the KGB/FSB/SVR. On the other hand, the KGB usually held pride of place in the Soviet intelligence hierarchy, and the GRU was often placed in a state of de facto subordination to the former. A number of GRU leaders, in fact, came from the KGB and its predecessors. For example, Ivan Serov, KGB chairman from 1954–1958, was demoted and sent to head the GRU from 1958–1963. In the more fractured post-Soviet environment, the GRU is now fully independent of the political security services.

The GRU in America: The Soviet Period

In the early years of the Soviet regime, according to historian Jonathan Haslam, "military intelligence seemed more promising than its civilian counterpart, both larger and more substantial." (Haslam, *Near and Distant Neighbors*, 23) Fueled by a culture of risk-taking inculcated by its most influential early leader, Yan Berzin, and heavily relying on recruitment of foreign communists, the GRU built overseas agent networks that equaled or surpassed those belonging to the KGB's predecessors, known by the mid-1930s as the NKVD. However, the GRU's risk-taking soon caught up to it, resulting in the exposure of several of its overseas networks. As a result, GRU was subordinated to the foreign intelligence branch of the NKVD, and many of its surviving networks were transferred to the latter.

Nonetheless, many of the GRU's earlier efforts continued to bear fruit in the mid-to-late 1930s. This was especially true in America, where the GRU succeeded in establishing a network of communist and pro-communist agents within the Roosevelt Administration from 1935–1938. Arguably the most important of these agents was Alger Hiss, a well-connected, up and coming, Harvard law graduate, who in September 1936 began working at the State Department. Hiss' GRU controller was an American, a communist party member, a writer and editor reassigned to underground work in 1932: Whittaker Chambers. Chambers in turn reported to the head of GRU operations in America, Col. Boris Bykov.

In April 1938, disillusioned by Stalin's Great Terror, then at its height, Chambers defected from the GRU and CPUSA. After more than a year spent hiding from Soviet intelligence, Chambers would take a job at Time Magazine, eventually becoming a senior editor.

By 1945, Hiss had become a senior State Department official, accompanying President Roosevelt to the Yalta conference in February, and organizing the opening conference of the United Nations in San Francisco. He was also still working for the GRU, under the code name "ALES.". A March 30, 1945 report from the NKVD station chief in Washington to Moscow noted that: "Ales has been continuously working with the neighbors (i.e. the GRU) since 1935." (Quoted in Haynes, Klehr, and Vassiliev, *Spies*, 20–21)

In August 1948, the House Un-American Activities Committee held hearings on communist espionage in the US Government. Somewhat reluctantly, Whittaker Chambers came forward to testify about his activities as a

Whittaker Chambers, 1948. An American communist and GRU agent during the 1930s, his famous testimony against Alger Hiss in 1948 would prove one of the most dramatic moments in HUAC's history. Library of Congress Prints & Photographs Division: https://www.loc.gov/item/95512199/

GRU agent in the 1930s. He named numerous individuals who had been part of his network, including Hiss. By now, Hiss had left the State Department to become president of the Carnegie Endowment and was a pillar of the New Deal establishment. He vehemently denied Chambers's accusations, and the confrontation between the two men became the focus of the HUAC investigation, spawning a bitter partisan controversy that dominated the headlines and would linger for decades. Eventually, Chambers produced copies of microfilmed documents that Hiss had given him. In 1950, Hiss was convicted of perjury for denying under oath his involvement with the GRU, and was sentenced to four years in prison. For five decades, Hiss was considered by many to be the victim of red-baiting hysteria, but post-Cold War archival revelations have largely validated Chambers's claims.

After World War II, the GRU largely played second fiddle to the NKVD/KGB in terms of Soviet intelligence activity in America. The main exception was during the John F. Kennedy Administration (1961–3), especially during the Cuban Missile Crisis of October 1962. A GRU Colonel named Georgi Bolshakov, working undercover as a news correspondent, maintained a back-door channel of communication with Attorney General Robert Kennedy that proved important in helping resolve the confrontation. Less happily for the Soviets, another GRU Colonel, Oleg Penkovsky played an equally crucial role. Arrested in Moscow in September 1962 as a spy, the information Penkovsky previously provided to the CIA helped reveal that the Soviets were installing ballistic missiles in Cuba, thus leading to the US blockade of the island.

The GRU in Post-Soviet Times: "Little Green Men" and "Fancy Bear"

Unlike the KGB, which was broken up into a number of separate organizations, the GRU survived the fall of Soviet communism intact. Its fortunes have waxed and waned in the quarter-century since the end of the USSR. After facing a potentially serious loss of prestige and status following its failures in Russia's 2008 war with Georgia, the GRU has come back with a vengeance this decade. It has reverted to the ambitious, risk-taking mentality of its early years that, in researcher Mark Galeotti's view, "reflects a war-time mindset." It has exploited its unique paramilitary capabilities, especially in Ukraine, where GRU was the main driving force behind the "little green

Lt. General Igor Korobov, head of the
GRU from 2016–2018, sanctioned by the
Obama Administration for the GRU's
role in the election-related hacking of
2016. Korobov died in November 2018.
Source: Russian Ministry of Defense
(mil.ru), via Wikipedia: https://
commons.wikimedia.org/wiki
/File:Igor_Korobov_(2016–02–01).jpg

men" who invaded Crimea and regions of eastern Ukraine in 2014. The GRU
has also shown a growing willingness to engage in paramilitary subversion
beyond the former Soviet Union. It has been implicated in a planned October 2016 coup against the pro-NATO government of Montenegro. GRU
agents have also been linked to a violent, radical right group in Hungary,
allegedly supplying them with both weapons and training.

The GRU's risk-taking, aggressive, war mentality transcends kinetic action.
It has also been applied in cyberspace, employing the tools of the digital age

to pursue espionage and influence operations. One of the world's most ambitious and highly effective hacking organizations, dubbed APT 28, or "Fancy Bear", is believed to be run by the GRU. It is through such cyber operations that the GRU has once again dramatically influenced events in the United States. According to US government and private analysts, it was Fancy Bear that conducted the most egregious of the 2016 election-related hacks here in the US, directed at the Democratic National Committee and other political targets.

The official unclassified US intelligence community report on the hacking, released in January, strongly emphasized the primary role of the GRU in carrying them out:

> The General Staff Main Intelligence Directorate (GRU) probably began cyber operations aimed at the US election by March 2016. We assess that the GRU operations resulted in the compromise of the personal e-mail accounts of Democratic Party officials and political figures. By May, the GRU had exfiltrated large volumes of data from the DNC.
>
> We assess with high confidence that the GRU relayed material it acquired from the DNC and senior Democratic officials to WikiLeaks. (Office of the Director, "Assessing Russian Activities," 2–3)

In response to the hacks of the DNC and other American political organizations, on December 29, 2016, the Obama Administration sanctioned the GRU "for tampering, altering, or causing a misappropriation of information with the purpose or effect of interfering with the 2016 U.S. election processes." (White House Office, "Fact Sheet") In addition, sanctions were imposed on GRU head Lt. General Igor Korobov and three of his deputies. The release announcing these sanctions likewise emphasized the leading role of the GRU in conducting the hacking.

Over three decades after the end of the Cold War, not only does the GRU continue to operate against America, but the impact of those operations is arguably greater than ever before.

Primary Congressional Sources Concerning the GRU

Conduct of Espionage Within the United States by Agents of Foreign Communist Governments: Hearings Before the Committee on Un-American Activities, House of Representatives, 90th Congress, First Session. 1967.

Hearings Regarding Communist Espionage in United States Government,
Part 1: Hearings Before the Committee on Un-American Activities, House of
Representatives, 80th Congress, Second Session. 1948.

Interim Report on Hearings Regarding Communist Espionage in United
States Government: Investigation of Un-American Activities in the United
States. Committee on Un-American Activities, House of Representatives, 80th
Congress, Second Session. 1948.

Investigation of Un-American Propaganda Activities in the United States,
Volume 9, Hearings before a Special Committee on Un-American Activities,
House of Representatives, 76th Congress, First Session. 1939.

The Kremlin's Espionage and Terror Organizations: Testimony of Petr S.
Deriabin, Former Officer of the USSR's Committee of State Security (KGB):
Hearing before the Committee on Un-American Activities, House of Represen-
tatives, 86th Congress, First Session. 1959.

Patterns of Communist Espionage: Report by the Committee on Un-Ameri-
can Activities, 80th Congress, Second Session. 1958.

Scope of Soviet Activity in the United States, Part 1: Hearing Before the Sub-
committee to Investigate the Administration of the Internal Security Act and
Other Internal Security Laws of the Committee on the Judiciary, United States
Senate, 84th Congress, Second Session. 1956.

The Shameful Years: Thirty Years of Soviet Espionage in the United States.
Committee on Un-American Activities, House of Representatives. 1951.

Soviet Espionage within United States Government: Second Report. Com-
mittee on Un-American Activities, 80th Congress, Second Session. 1948.

Further Primary Sources

Cold War International History Project. Venona Project and Vassiliev Notebooks
     Index and Concordance. https://www.wilsoncenter.org/article/venona
     -project-and-vassiliev-notebooks-index-and-concordance.
Office of the Director of National Intelligence. "Assessing Russian Activities and
     Intentions in Recent US Elections." January 6, 2017. https://www.dni.gov/files
     /documents/ICA_2017_01.pdf.
White House Office of the Press Secretary. "FACT SHEET: Actions in Response
     to Russian Malicious Cyber Activity and Harassment." December 29, 2016.
     https://obamawhitehouse.archives.gov/the-press-office/2016/12/29
     /fact-sheet-actions-response-russian-malicious-cyber-activity-and.

Additional Sources

Andrew, Christopher and Vasili Mitrokhin. *The Sword and the Shield: The Mitrokhin Archive and the Secret History of the KGB.* New York: Basic Books, 1999.

Frenkel, Sheera. "Meet Fancy Bear." *Buzzfeed News,* October 15, 2016. https://www.buzzfeednews.com/article/sheerafrenkel/meet-fancy-bear-the-russian-group-hacking-the-us-election.

Galeotti, Mark. *Putin's Hydra: Inside Russia's Intelligence Services.* European Council on Foreign Relations, May 11, 2016. https://ecfr.eu/publication/putins_hydra_inside_russias_intelligence_services/.

Haslam, Jonathan. *Near and Distant Neighbors: A New History of Soviet Intelligence.* New York: Farrar, Straus and Giroux, 2015.

Haynes, John Earl, Harvey Klehr and Alexander Vassiliev. *Spies: The Rise and Fall of the KGB in America.* New Haven: Yale University Press, 2009.

Leonard, Raymond W. *Secret Soldiers of the Revolution: Soviet Military Intelligence, 1918–1933.* Westport Conn.: Greenwood Press, 1999.

Suvorov, Victor. *Inside Soviet Military Intelligence.* New York: Macmillan, 1984.

Suvorov, Victor. *Inside the Aquarium: The Making of a Top Soviet Spy.* New York: Macmillan, 1986.

Walker, Shaun. "US expulsions put spotlight on Russia's GRU intelligence agency." *The Guardian,* December 30, 2016. https://www.theguardian.com/world/2016/dec/30/us-expulsions-put-spotlight-on-russias-gru-intelligence-agency?CMP=share_btn_tw.

Weiss, Michael. "The GRU: Putin's No-Longer-So-Secret Weapon." *The Daily Beast,* December 31, 2016. https://www.thedailybeast.com/the-gru-putins-no-longer-so-secret-weapon.

3

"False Alarm"

Communist Allegations of Biological Warfare in the Korean War

O NE CONSEQUENCE OF THE COVID-19 pandemic has been the numerous charges and counter-charges regarding the origins of the virus. In particular, the allegations by the Trump administration that the pandemic was the result of research done at a scientific laboratory in Wuhan, China that then leaked out. Both China and Russia have countered with claims that the COVID pandemic was actually created, purposefully or not, by the United States.

Such competing political claims regarding the origins of diseases are nothing new. They were, in fact, a regular staple of the Cold War information and propaganda contest. The USSR and its allies from the early 1950s regularly blamed domestic diseases and crop failures on American efforts at biological warfare (BW). Most famously, the 1980s KGB active measures campaign "Operation Denver" claimed that the AIDS virus was created at a U.S. Army biological research facility at Fort Detrick, MD. In turn the U.S. alleged that a 1979 anthrax outbreak in the Soviet city of Sverdlovsk was the result of a biological warfare accident (true), and that in the early 1980s the USSR used a mycotoxin dubbed "yellow rain" in Afghanistan and Southeast Asia (unproven: likely false.)

The earliest major Cold War controversy involving allegations of BW was a series of claims by China and North Korea in 1951–52 that the United States employed biological weapons during the Korean War. While vehemently denied by the US, these charges were treated as credible by much of the left in Western Europe, and by a large part of what would soon become known as the Third World. Most western scholars have rejected the allegations, noting that credible

evidence of US BW use is lacking. Post-Cold War Soviet and Chinese revelations, in particular, have cast tremendous doubt on the communist charges.

Unit 731 and the Origins of the Campaign

It is difficult to understand the Korean War BW controversy without putting it in the context of Japan's WWII biological weapons program. Imperial Japan had an extensive BW program between 1932–45, with its largest,
most infamous element, Unit 731, located in Manchuria, directly north of the
Korean peninsula. According to scholar Sheldon H. Harris, Japan's horrific
BW activities, both gruesome experiments and actual use of bacteriological
weapons, killed some 250,000 people in China and Manchuria. After the war,
many of the leading figures in Japan's BW program were captured by American occupation authorities. This included the longtime head of Unit 731,
General Shiro Ishii. Shamefully, the American authorities granted Ishii and
his colleagues immunity from prosecution, in return for providing US intelligence with the results of their research.

In contrast, the USSR, in December 1949 staged a trial at Khabarovsk in
the Soviet Far East, in which 12 captured Japanese officers tied to Unit 731
were tried for war crimes. On the one hand, the trial did much to expose the
terrible truth of Japan's BW program. However, it was also a propaganda event
designed to embarrass the United States and Japan. In addition to noting that
Ishii and his colleagues were protected by the U.S., the Soviets claimed that
Ishii was continuing his BW efforts at American behest, and even demanded
the extradition of Emperor Hirohito for complicity in Unit 731's activities.

The crimes of Unit 731 played a key part in the communist allegations of
American BW use in Korea. Many of the reported biological attacks directly
matched Japanese methods used during WW II. In addition, Unit 731 was
prominently featured in communist propaganda even before the first allegations of American bacteriological warfare were made. In the words of scholar
Milton Leitenberg:

> In the first five months of 1951, the Chinese press and radio made repea-
> ted references to Gen. Ishii and the Japanese wartime BW programs, the
> Khabarovsk trial, Gen. Ishii's subsequent employment by the United
> States, and the claim that the United States was preparing to use BW in
> the Korean War. (Leitenberg, "New Russian Evidence," 188)

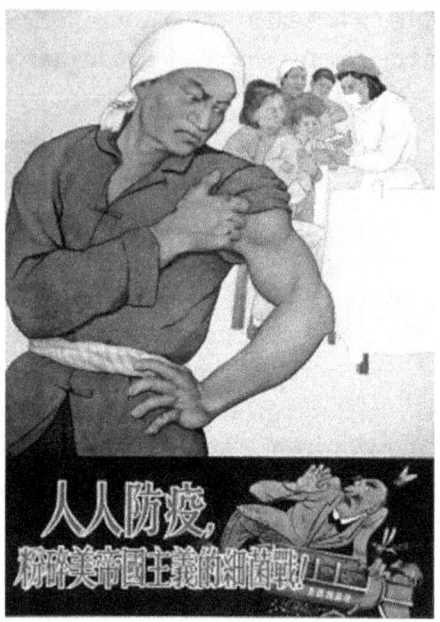

"Chinese propaganda poster from the
Korean War era: "Vaccinate everyone,
to crush the germ warfare of American
imperialism!"" Image via Wikipedia:
https://en.wikipedia.org/wiki/File:1950s
_Chinese_propaganda_poster_against
_American_biowarfare.jpg

Two Waves of Charges

The Korean War began on June 25, 1950, when communist North Korea invaded pro-western South Korea. As noted above, after communist China entered the war in late 1950 to save North Korea from defeat, Chinese media
outlets offered frequent warnings that the US was preparing to resort to BW.
It was not until May 8, 1951, that the first allegation of actual BW use was
made, when North Korea's foreign minister accused the US of having spread
smallpox in parts of North Korea. Occasional Chinese and North Korean
claims of American biological weapons use continued into the summer of
1951. In addition to BW, the Chinese also claimed during this period that US
forces employed poison gas.

The main communist campaign claiming that America was using BW came
in the winter and spring of 1952. On February 22, 1952, the North Korean

Foreign Minister once again accused the United States of using biological weapons. This time, the allegations were that American planes dropped a variety of insects over North Korea, carrying diseases such as plague, anthrax, and cholera. The methods described were virtually identical to those used by the Japanese in China during WWII. The charges were soon echoed by the Chinese, who claimed that US aircraft were engaged in such activities over both North Korea and northeast China, with American planes allegedly flying about 1,000 BW-related sorties over the latter region between January-March 1952. As evidence, the Chinese produced insects they claimed were dropped from US aircraft, American leaflet bombs that they claimed had been used to deliver these insects, and coerced interrogations from several dozen captured American airmen.

By-mid March, the two communist countries, joined by their patron the Soviet Union, had embarked on a massive propaganda campaign based on the BW charges. The Soviets, through their front organization the World Peace Council, stirred up anti-American sentiment in western Europe and elsewhere. China, while spurning offers of an investigation by the International Red Cross or World Health Organization, assembled two investigative committees composed of sympathetic individuals that released reports supporting the communist allegations. Within China, the Maoist regime used the hysteria whipped up by the BW charges to launch a "patriotic hygiene" campaign that mobilized much of the Chinese population in support of a sweeping vaccination and public health effort.

Starting in early March, the United States vehemently denied the communist allegations. The biological warfare controversy began to fade by the fall of 1952, and soon became a historical footnote with the Korean War armistice of May 1953.

Recent Revelations

Since the Korean War, the question of whether the United States engaged in biological warfare has occasionally fostered controversy. China and North Korea insist to this day that the BW allegations were true. Most western historians disagree. A small group of radical left western scholars have periodically tried to validate the communist charges and prove the US guilty of employing BW in Korea. The most recent effort in this regard is writer Nicholson Baker's 2020 book *Baseless*. The book summarizes the case for American guilt, but is ultimately shoddy and unconvincing.

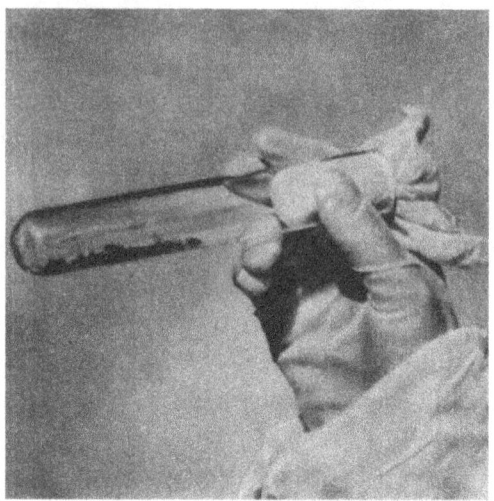

"Chinese photograph of infected fleas
allegedly spread by the United States" Image
via Wikimedia Commons: https://commons.
wikimedia.org/wiki/File:1952–03_%E6%9C%
9D%E9%B2%9C%E6%88%98%E4%BA%89%
E7%BE%8E%E5%86%9B%E6%8A%95%E6%9
4%BE%E5%B8%A6%E6%9C%89%E7%BB%8
6%E8%8F%8C%E7%9A%84%E8%B7%B3%E8
%9A%A4.png

The bulk of the evidence strongly indicates that the communist charges are false if not outright fabricated. For one thing, there is no direct documentary evidence that America tried to employ BW in Korea, While the US did have a biological warfare program at the time, scholars such as Conrad Crane have shown that America lacked the ability to wage a campaign such as the Chinese and North Koreans alleged. Also, there were no actual widespread epidemics reported in China, and none in North Korea that couldn't be explained by natural methods of disease spread. The only evidence produced in support of the charges was by the communists themselves. The "confessions" by American POWs were repudiated as soon as those men returned to the United States.

The most conclusive evidence refuting the communist allegations emerged in the 1990s from China and the former Soviet Union. In 1997, Wu Zhili, the head of medical services for Chinese forces during the Korean War, wrote a brief memoir reflecting on his 1952 investigation of alleged US BW use. Discovered after his death in 2008, the document was published in a Chinese publication in 2013:

(1) Imperialism is capable of carrying out all manner of evils, and bacteriological war is not an exception. (2) Severe winter, however, is not a good season for conducting bacteriological war. When the weather is cold the mobility of insects is weakened, and is not conducive to bacteria reproduction. (3) Dropping [objects] on the front line trenches, where there are few people and sickness does not spread easily, and where the U.S. military's trenches are not more than ten meters away, allows for the possibility of ricocheting. (4) Korea already had an epidemic of lice-borne contagious diseases. All the houses in the cities and towns had been burned down, and the common people all lived in air-raid shelters. Their lives are already difficult, but the Korean people are extremely tenacious and bacteriological warfare cannot be the greater disaster that forces them to surrender. (5) Our preliminary investigation still could not prove that the U.S. military carried out bacteriological warfare. ("Wu Zhili, 'The Bacteriological War of 1952 is a False Alarm'")

In conclusion, Wu wrote, "the bacteriological war of 1952 was a false alarm."

Even more damning, in 1998 a Japanese newspaper obtained copies of a number of high-level Soviet documents from April and May 1953 concerning the Korean War BW allegations. The documents show that the senior leadership of the Soviet Communist Party, who had just taken power after the March 1953 death of Joseph Stalin, quickly and unabashedly labeled the allegations as fabricated. Perhaps the most important document is a May 2, 1953 message from the new Soviet leadership directly to Mao Tse-Tung:

The Soviet Government and the Central Committee of the CPSU were misled. The spread in the press of information about the use by the Americans of bacteriological weapons in Korea was based on false information. The accusations against the Americans were fictitious. ("Resolution of the Presidium of the USSR Council of Ministers")

While it appears that the Chinese and North Koreans may have genuinely believed in early 1952 that the United States was using BW against them, they soon realized that this was not the case. Nonetheless, they cynically continued making the charges, for purposes of international propaganda and domestic mobilization. This would be only one of many such situations during the Cold War in which real and fictitious incidents of disease and BW activity would become tools of global political warfare.

Sources

Baker, Nicholson. *Baseless: My Search for Truth in the Ruins of the Freedom of Information Act*. New York: Penguin Press, 2020.

Crane, Conrad C. "'No Practical Capabilities': American Biological and Chemical Warfare Programs During the Korean War," *Perspectives in Biology and Medicine 45*, no. 2 (Spring 2002): 241–249. DOI: 0.1353/pbm.2002.0024.

Harris, Sheldon H. *Factories of Death: Japanese Biological Warfare, 1932–1945, and the American Cover-Up*. New York: Routledge, 2002.

Jager, Sheila Miyoshi. *Brothers at War: The Unending Conflict in Korea*. New York: W. W. Norton & Company, 2013.

Leitenberg, Milton. "China's False Allegations of the Use of Biological Weapons by the United States during the Korean War." Cold War International History Project Working Paper #78, March 2016. https://www.wilsoncenter.org/publication/chinas-false-allegations-the-use-biological-weapons-the-united-states-during-the-korean.

Leitenberg, Milton. "New Russian Evidence on the Korean War Biological Warfare Allegations: Background and Analysis." *Cold War International History Project Bulletin 11* (Winter 1998): 180–199. https://www.wilsoncenter.org/sites/default/files/media/documents/publication/CWIHP_Bulletin_11.pdf.

Materials on the Trial of Former Servicemen of the Japanese Army Charged with Manufacturing and Employing Bacteriological Weapons. Moscow: Foreign Languages Publishing House, 1950.

Regis, Ed. *The Biology of Doom: The History of America's Secret Germ Warfare Project*. New York: Henry Holt, 1999.

"Resolution of the Presidium of the USSR Council of Ministers about Letters to the Ambassador of the USSR in the PRC, V.V. Kuznetsov and to the Charge d'Affaires for the USSR in the DPRK, S.P. Suzdalev," May 02, 1953, History and Public Policy Program Digital Archive, Archive of the President of the Russian Federation. Translated by Kathryn Weathersby. https://digitalarchive.wilsoncenter.org/document/112030.

"Wu Zhili, 'The Bacteriological War of 1952 is a False Alarm'," September 1997, History and Public Policy Program Digital Archive, *Yanhuang chunqiu* no. 11 (2013): 36–39. Translated by Drew Casey. https://digitalarchive.wilsoncenter.org/document/123080.

4

"The Crime and the Lie"

The Katyn Forest Massacre, 1940

Major Baruch Steinberg (1897–1940), chief
rabbi of the Polish Army at the start of World
War II. Major Steinberg was one of over 40
Polish military chaplains among the more
than 21,000 Poles murdered at Katyn and
elsewhere in April-May 1940. Source: United
States Holocaust Memorial Museum. https://
collections.ushmm.org/search/catalog/pa12479

IN SEPTEMBER 1939, MAJOR Baruch Steinberg served as the chief rabbi of the Polish Army. Sadly, few will be surprised to learn that Major Steinberg was brutally murdered in the wake of the German invasion of Poland that month. After all, an estimated 3,000,000 Polish Jews were eventually murdered in the Holocaust. What may come as a surprise is that it was not the Nazis who killed Major Steinberg. Rather, it was the other totalitarian power that invaded Poland in September 1939, the Soviet Union, that murdered him, along with over 21,000 other Poles over the course of April and May 1940.

On September 1, 1939, Nazi Germany invaded Poland to mark the beginning of the Second World War in Europe. On September 17, 1939, the Soviet Union, in alliance with the Germans, invaded Poland from the east. Under the terms of the Molotov-Ribbentrop Pact of August 23, 1939, the Third Reich and USSR agreed to partition eastern Europe between themselves. The Soviets gained control of the eastern half of Poland, plus the Baltic states of Lithuania, Latvia and Estonia; the regions of Bessarabia and northern Bukovina from Romania; and parts of Finland obtained as a result of the "Winter War" of November 1939– March 1940.

In all, the Soviet portion of occupied Poland contained over 77,000 square miles of Polish territory, with a population of over 12 million people, constituting over half of pre-war Poland's land and nearly 40% of its population. All of these lands were annexed to the Soviet Union. The Soviet occupation also exacted a devastating human toll. At least 30,000 Poles were killed in a series of mass executions, Over half a million other Poles were imprisoned or deported to the Gulag system of forced labor camps or to special settlements in Siberia or central Asia. An estimated 90,000–100,000 Poles died during these deportations. (Paczkowski, "Poland, the 'Enemy Nation,'" 372; Kochanski, *The Eagle Unbowed*, 137–38) The most infamous Soviet atrocity against Poland is what became known as the Katyn Forest Massacre.

The Katyn Massacre

In the course of their invasion, the Soviets are estimated to have captured 240,000 Polish troops. While many of the enlisted men were released, over 14,000 Polish officers, along with police, border guards, officials and others, were kept in custody. They were dispatched to three major prison camps: Kozelsk, in western Russia; Starobelsk, in present-day Ukraine; and

Ostashkov, northwest of Moscow. The camps were under the control of the Soviet secret police, known then as the NKVD.

For approximately five months, the Polish prisoners were subjected to Soviet propaganda and interrogated on their attitudes toward the USSR while the Soviets considered what to do with them. By early March, the Soviet authorities had come to a decision. On March 5, 1940, Lavrenty Beria, head of the NKVD, sent a memorandum to Soviet dictator Josef Stalin that sealed the fate of the prisoners:

> In the USSR NKVD prisoner-of-war camps and prisons of the western regions of Ukraine and Belorussia, there are at present a large number of former officers of the Polish Army, former workers in the Polish police and intelligence organs, members of Polish nationalist c-r parties ... and others. They are all sworn enemies of Soviet power, filled with hatred for the Soviet system of government. (Quoted in Cienciala, *Katyn*, 118)

According to Beria, there were a total of 14,736 prisoners held in the three camps. Beria recommended that these men (only one was a woman), along with 11,000 Polish prisoners held in NKVD prisons, be dealt with via "the supreme measure of punishment, [execution by] shooting." (Quoted in ibid., 120)

Beria's recommendation was unanimously approved by Stalin and the Politburo. Beginning on April 3, groups of prisoners from each of the three camps were taken to special NKVD execution facilities and shot. By the time the operation ran its course in late May 1940, the NKVD had killed 14,552 of the Poles held at Kozelsk, Ostashkov, and Starobelsk, along with 7,305 additional victims held in regular NKVD prisons. Major Steinberg, along with over 40 other Polish military chaplains, would be among those murdered. The families of those executed were rounded up by the NKVD and deported to special settlements in Kazakhstan, where many died in difficult conditions.

In April 1943, the Germans discovered the site in the Katyn Forest, near the Russian city of Smolensk, where the Kozelsk prisoners were murdered, and announced the discovery to the world. The Soviets denied the German charges, and declared that the Nazis were responsible for the crime. Not until 1990 did the USSR admit responsibility for murdering the Polish prisoners. While only about 20% of the overall number of victims were killed at Katyn, the entire mass killing has become known as the Katyn Forest Massacre. Despite occasional attempts at reconciliation, Katyn continues to haunt Russo-Polish relations to the present day.

Sources on Katyn

Cienciala, Anna M., Natalia S. Lebedeva, and Wojciech Materski. *Katyn: A Crime Without Punishment*. New Haven: Yale University Press, 2007.

Fischer, Benjamin B. "The Katyn Controversy: Stalin's Killing Field." *Studies in Intelligence*, Winter 1999–2000. https://www.cia.gov/static /5a3e46e77b3c417a15bcf927e7b049cc/Stalins-Killing-Field.pdf.

The Katyn Forest Massacre. Hearings before the Select Committee to Conduct an Investigation of the Facts, Evidence and Circumstances of the Katyn Forest Massacre, Eighty-Second Congress, First[-Second] Session. 7 vols. 1952.

Paczkowski, Andrzej."Poland, 'The Enemy Nation'." in Stephane Courtois and Mark Kramer (eds.) *The Black Book of Communism: Crimes, Terror, Repression*. Cambridge, MA: Harvard University Press, 1999.

Paul, Allen. *Katyn: Stalin's Massacre and the Triumph of Truth*. DeKalb: Northern Illinois University Press, 2010.

Snyder, Timothy. *Bloodlands: Europe Between Hitler and Stalin*. New York: Basic Books, 2010.

Additional Sources

The Avalon Project. "Nazi-Soviet Relations 1939–1941." Yale University Law School. https://avalon.law.yale.edu/subject_menus/nazsov.asp.

Foreign Relations of the United States: The Soviet Union, 1933–1939. Washington, DC: Government Printing Office, 1952.

Foreign Relations of the United States, 1941: Volume I: General, The Soviet Union. Washington, DC: Government Printing Office, 1958.

Gross, Jan Tomasz. *Revolution from Abroad: The Soviet Conquest of Poland's Western Ukraine and Western Belorussia*. Expanded ed. Princeton: Princeton University Press, 2002.

Kochanski, Halik. *The Eagle Unbowed: Poland and the Poles in the Second World War*. Cambridge, MA: Harvard University Press, 2012.

United States Holocaust Memorial Museum. "German-Soviet Pact." *Holocaust Encyclopedia*. https://encyclopedia.ushmm.org/content/en/article/german -soviet-pact.

5

Congress Investigates the Katyn Forest Massacre, 1951–1952

Rep. Ray Madden (D-IN) (1892–1987),
chairman of the House Select Committee to
Investigate the Katyn Forest Massacre. Source:
Wikipedia. http://commons.wikimedia
.org/wiki/File:Ray_Madden_%2892nd
_Congress%29.jpg

I N THE SPRING OF 1940, the Soviet secret police, known as the NKVD, would murder nearly 22,000 Polish prisoners, many of them army officers or policemen, in what became known as the Katyn Forest Massacre. In 1943, after the Germans found one of the major killing sites, in western Russia's Katyn Forest, and gleefully exploited it for their own propaganda purposes, the Soviets denied responsibility for the atrocity and instead blamed it on the Germans. As then allies of the USSR, the US government accepted the Soviet explanation and refused to support the demands of the Polish government-in-exile for an independent investigation. Even after the end of World War II, when US-Soviet relations deteriorated with the start of the Cold War, the American government made no effort to reopen the Katyn issue. Only the efforts of Polish exiles and Polish-American organizations, in alliance with certain journalists and prominent anti-communists such as Julius Epstein and Arthur Bliss Lane, kept the Katyn question alive in America.

By 1951, the activist campaign to encourage an official American investigation of Katyn was gaining traction. Amplified by the fact that America was at war against communist forces in Korea, and fears that American POWs would meet a fate similar to those of the Polish POWs at Katyn, Congress showed a willingness to conduct its own investigation of Katyn. On September 18, 1951, the House of Representatives voted 398–0 in support of House Resolution 390, which "provided for the establishment of a select committee to conduct a full and complete investigation concerning the Katyn massacre, an international crime committed against soldiers and citizens of Poland at the beginning of World War II." (*Final Report*, 1)

The House Select Committee to Conduct an Investigation of the Facts, Evidence and Circumstances of the Katyn Forest Massacre consisted of seven members, four Democrats and three Republicans. All seven committee members came from the Northeast or upper Midwest, and represented districts with large Polish-American populations. In all, the committee included members from Michigan (2), Wisconsin, Illinois, Indiana, Pennsylvania, and Massachusetts. The committee was unofficially known as the "Madden Committee," after its chair, Rep. Ray Madden. Madden, a Democrat, represented Indiana's First Congressional District, centered around the industrial city of Gary.

The Madden Committee held hearings from October 1951–November 1952. It interviewed 81 witnesses, produced 183 exhibits, and took over 100 depositions. It was the first congressional committee to hold hearings over-seas, meeting with witnesses in London, Frankfurt, Berlin, and Naples. Ulti-mately, it would produce 7 volumes worth of hearings, numbering 2,362 pages.

The Madden Committee published an interim report in July 1952, fol-lowed by its final report in December 1952. Among its major findings, the committee unanimously concluded that the NKVD committed the Katyn murders. As the committee's final report stated:

> On the basis of voluminous testimony, including that of recognized medical expert witnesses, and other data assembled by our staff, this committee concluded there does not exist a scintilla of proof, or even any remote circumstantial evidence, that this mass murder took place no later than the spring of 1940. The Poles were then prisoners of the Soviets and the Katyn Forest area was still under Soviet occupation. (*Final Report*, 2)

In light of its finding of Soviet guilt for Katyn, the committee recommended that the US government pursue charges against the Soviets before the Inter-national World Court of Justice at The Hague.

The Madden Committee's most controversial findings concerned the response of the Roosevelt Administration to the news of the Katyn discov-ery in 1943. It concluded that, out of a desire to preserve the wartime alliance with the USSR, the US government overlooked or deliberately suppressed information pointing to Soviet guilt for Katyn. Specifically, in 1945 Presi-dent Roosevelt personally intervened to have the Navy transfer an officer to American Samoa in order to prevent him from going public with his concerns about Katyn. In addition, the Chief of Army Intelligence suppressed a report by a former American POW who had been taken to Katyn by the Germans in 1943, and had reluctantly concluded that the Soviets were guilty. Finally, the Madden Committee established that the Office of War Information had coerced Polish-language radio stations in Detroit and Buffalo to cease their coverage of the Katyn allegations.

Historians who have studied Katyn have noted that the Madden Com-mittee's investigation was flawed in several ways. For one, it invited several witnesses whose testimony was proven to be unreliable. One in particular was an anonymous witness designated "John Doe," who wore a hood and testified that he saw Poles being murdered at Katyn in November 1939, an allegation that flies in the face of all the available evidence. In addition, the Madden Committee was, almost unavoidably, caught up in the broader controversies over McCarthyism and domestic anti-Communism. Finally, its recommendation that the Soviets be brought before the World Court for Katyn was ignored by the incoming Eisenhower Administration and soon forgotten.

Despite these flaws, however, the Madden Committee served a valuable role in both the history and memory of Katyn. It firmly established Soviet responsibility for Katyn in the historical record, and its major conclusions have been vindicated by subsequent scholarship. In the words of historian Alexander Etkind and his co-authors, "The Madden Committee's resounding verdict of Soviet guilt for the crime of Katyn was a central memory event." (Etkind, *Remembering Katyn*, 22) Similarly, Allen Paul has written that "on the whole the Select Committee went about its work in a methodical, workman-like manner. Like a skillful prosecutor, it carefully assembled its case; and when the facts were all laid out, the overall results were impressive." (Paul, *Katyn*, 340)

It was not until 1990, when Soviet communism was in its death throes, that the USSR would finally admit that it had perpetrated the Katyn massacre. In 2000, the Polish parliament (Sejm) passed a resolution thanking the Madden Committee, among others, for its efforts in establishing the truth about Katyn. (Sanford, *Katyn and the Soviet Massacre*, 218).

Primary Sources

*The Katyn Forest Massacre. Final Report of the Select Committee to Conduct
    an Investigation of the Facts, Evidence and Circumstances of the Katyn Forest
    Massacre*, December 22, 1952.
*The Katyn Forest Massacre. Hearings before the Select Committee to Conduct
    an Investigation of the Facts, Evidence and Circumstances of the Katyn Forest
    Massacre, Eighty-Second Congress, First[-Second] Session.* 7 vols. 1952.

Additional Sources

Etkind, Alexander, Rory Finnin, et al. *Remembering Katyn*. Cambridge, UK:
    Polity Press, 2012.
Paul, Allen. *Katyn: Stalin's Massacre and the Triumph of Truth*. DeKalb: Northern
    Illinois University Press, 2010.
Sanford, George. *Katyn and the Soviet Massacre of 1940: Truth, Justice and
    Memory*. London; New York: Routledge, 2005.

6

Previewing the Film Katyn

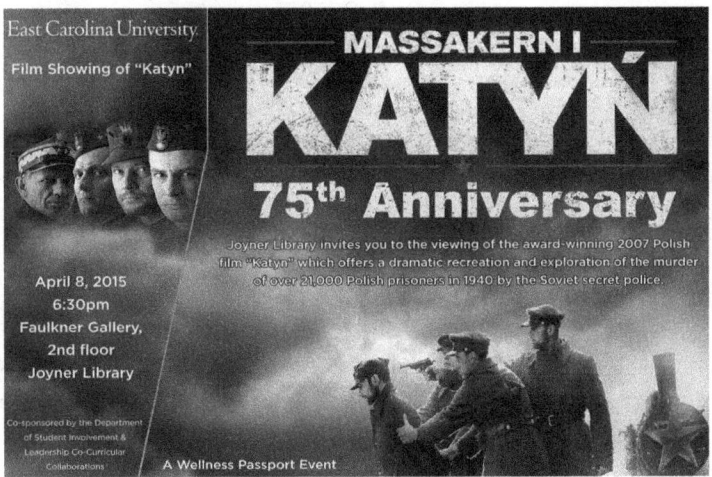

"BUT THE FIRST FILM had to show the crime – and the lie. The crime: that was indeed my father who was murdered there. The lie: my mother was one of the ladies who was constantly trying to find information, she was writing to the Red Cross in London and Switzerland, she clung on to the hope that her husband would return from the war. She was lied to that he didn't die in Katyń, and only gradually did we discover the truth. We learnt that there were other camps, and those camps were also liquidated. In short, we learnt about the machinery of death."

Andrzej Wajda, quoted in *The Krakow Post*, June 19, 2009.

In 2015, Joyner Library, in acknowledgement of the 75th anniversary of the Katyn Forest Massacre, hosted a screening of the award-winning 2007 Polish film *Katyn*. This post offered a preview of the film. Considering the role that competing memories of the Second World War, and Katyn in particular, have played in producing the current conflict between Russia and its neighbors, this entry was left in despite perhaps being a little out of place.

The Context

The film *Katyn* is directed by Andrzej Wajda (1926–2016), a highly-acclaimed filmmaker who directed some 40 films in a career spanning six decades. Wajda's contributions as a director would be recognized in 2000 with an Academy Award for Lifetime Achievement, an honor for which he was nominated by Steven Spielberg. *Katyn* would be the fourth of Wajda's films to be nominated for the Oscar for Best Foreign Language Film.

Katyn was a deeply personal film for Wajda, one that he spent decades hoping he could make, yet doubting that he would ever be permitted to. Among the 21,857 Poles murdered at the behest of Josef Stalin in April-May 1940 was Wajda's father Jakub, a captain in the Polish army. Only 14 years old at the time, Wajda watched how his mother was consumed by years of grief and uncertainty. Communist authorities in Poland suppressed almost all discussion of the Katyn atrocities, especially if they hinted at Soviet guilt. Finally, the fall of the Soviet empire in eastern Europe in 1989 made it possible to openly discuss the Katyn massacre without fear of official repercussions. In addition, Soviet admission of guilt for Katyn in 1990, followed by the unraveling of the USSR, revealed many previously unknown facts about the killing operation of April-May 1940.

Eight decades later, the Katyn Forest Massacre remains a highly-charged symbol of historical memory that shapes the distrustful way many Poles, Lithuanians, Latvians, Estonians, and Ukrainians view Russia. It is an integral part of the current struggle over the history of World War II in eastern Europe, in which Russia portrays itself as the heroic liberator of Poland and the Baltic states from the Nazis, while the latter see themselves as victims of

Soviet oppression and occupation. Wajda's film has become a key part of this struggle, a cinematic symbol of the numerous Soviet deportations and mass killing actions during the 1930s and 1940s conducted in the region that historian Timothy Snyder has called the "Bloodlands". Both Ukraine and Estonia have honored Wajda for his achievement in making *Katyn*.

While keeping this context in mind, it is important to note that Wajda's *Katyn* is not an anti-Russian film. It even includes a sympathetic Russian character in the form of a Soviet army officer who saves the wife and daughter of the main Polish protagonist from the secret police. In April 2010, the film was shown twice on Russian television in a gesture of reconciliation, and Russia even presented Wajda with the Order of Friendship in December of that year.

The Film

While *Katyn* is a deeply personal film, it is not autobiographical. The film is strongly rooted in the historical record; however, the characters themselves are fictional archetypes who represent broader themes and ideas. The specific events portrayed in the film, while in accord with historical scholarship, are there at least in part for their symbolic value. For example, the film's opening sequence set on the bridge, where one crowd of terror-stricken Poles flees east to escape the Nazis, only to encounter another, equally terrified crowd fleeing west from the advancing Soviets.

Most of the film is not spent on the massacre itself, but rather on the impact of the atrocity and subsequent Soviet cover-up on the families and friends of those murdered. After the Soviets drive the Nazis from Poland in 1945, the characters in the film are confronted with a terrible dilemma: either to be part of the building of a "new" Poland, albeit on Soviet terms and requiring them to accept the Soviet lie that their loved ones were murdered by the Germans; or, to insist on telling the truth about what happened at Katyn, at the risk of marginalization or worse.

Finally, after taking us through 1945, Wajda uses the device of a recovered diary to take us back to April 1940 and show in stark, unsparing fashion the fate of those taken by the Soviet secret police into the Katyn Forest. In Wajda's view, giving the viewer a window on the killings was a necessity. As he told the *Krakow Post* in July 2009, "For the first film, I had to show the crime and its consequences." (Hodge, "Katyn")

As Alexander Etkind and his fellow authors have noted, most historical films have uplifting endings. (Etkind, *Remembering Katyn*, 49–50) Even a film as harrowing as *Schindler's List* gradually lifts the audience out of the horrors into which they have been submerged for most of the film. Wajda's *Katyn* grants the audience no such luxury. It ends with the horrifying spectacle of the Katyn executions. It is left to the audience to supply its own "happy" ending: to note that the very film they are watching is a reminder that Poland would ultimately shed Soviet domination; that the truth about Katyn would eventually prevail; that Wajda was, in fact, able to make the film he needed to make, showing both the crime that claimed the life of his father, and the lie that consumed his mother.

Sources

Etkind, Alexander, Rory Finnin, et al. *Remembering Katyn*. Cambridge, UK: Polity Press, 2012.

Hodge, Nick. "Andrzej Wajda on Katyń: The Full Transcript." *Krakow Post*, June 23, 2009. (Available via Internet Archive) https://web.archive.org /web/20130316142314/http:/www.krakowpost.com/article/1388.

Hodge, Nick. "Katyń: An Interview with Director Andrzej Wajda." *Krakow Post*, June 19, 2009. (Available via Internet Archive) https://web.archive.org /web/20130315051200/http:/www.krakowpost.com/article/1381.

Wajda.pl. "Katyn." (Available via Internet Archive) https://web.archive.org /web/20140708033732/http:/www.wajda.pl/en/filmy/katyn.html.

PART FIVE

Echoes and Legacies

*Countersubversion and Disinformation
from the Late Cold War to Present*

Congress Investigates Right-Wing Extremism,
From the 1960s to Present

I N THE LAST SEVERAL years, the rise of domestic right-wing extremism, in the form of the "alt-right" or white nationalism, has become a major issue in American politics. Events such as the violent "Unite the Right" rally in Charlottesville, VA in August 2017, the October 2018 Pittsburgh synagogue massacre, and the August 2019 racist mass shooting in El Paso, TX prompted congressional committees to hold a number of hearings investigating white nationalism and white supremacy.

This is not the first time that Congress has sought to investigate violent right-wing extremism. Such efforts can be traced all the way back to the inquiry into the first Ku Klux Klan in 1871–2. More recent examples of such investigations, focused on the Ku Klux Klan in the 1960s, and the militia movement in the 1990s, provide a degree of historical perspective on the current far right threat, as well as on efforts to understand and combat it.

HUAC Investigates the Klan, 1965–1966

In the post-World War II period, the House Un-American Activities Committee confined itself to investigating the Communist Party USA and other perceived sources of left-wing subversion. By the mid-1960s, however, with the civil rights revolution at its height, and the spread of segregationist terrorism and intimidation in response, the committee was left with little choice but to begin an investigation into the Ku Klux Klan (KKK).

HUAC began examining the KKK in the spring of 1965. A special subcommittee held public hearings from October 19, 1965 to February 24, 1966, and published a final report in December 1967. The committee found that

The Klan welcomes visitors to Greenville, n.d. Image courtesy of ECU Digital
Collections: http://digital.lib.ecu.edu/23542

there were a number of separate Klan organizations in the United States, of
which the United Klans of America (UKA) was the largest and most powerful. The UKA had by far its largest presence in North Carolina, where
it filled the space left by the white establishment's unwillingness to openly
oppose desegregation, as it did in states such as Alabama and Mississippi.
HUAC's investigation confirmed this, as committee investigator Philip Man-
uel revealed that there were an estimated 112 UKA klaverns (local chapters)
in North Carolina, making it, in his words, "by far the most active state in
terms of Klaverns and membership of the UKA." (*Activities of Ku Klux Klan
in the U.S.*, pt. 1, 1553)

The UKA was especially strong in eastern North Carolina. Of the 112
local Klan chapters, seven were found in Pitt County. Each of the counties

adjacent to Pitt also contained at least one UKA klavern (Lenoir County had five). As a result, a number of witnesses with ties to Greenville and Pitt County appeared before HUAC. This was the only HUAC investigation that focused on the eastern part of North Carolina.

In the wake of the HUAC investigation, the UKA soon went into decline, especially in North Carolina. By the end of the 1960s, the organization had been thoroughly marginalized. Some scholars have questioned the impact of HUAC's investigation in bringing about the demise of the UKA. Researcher David Cunningham has argued, however, that it played an important role in generating unwelcome publicity about the extent of UKA influence in North Carolina, in particular producing headlines that embarrassed the state's political and business elites, and thus prompted authorities in Raleigh to crack down on the organization.

The 1990s: Militias and Oklahoma City

The 1990s saw a further wave of concern regarding right-wing extremism. The spread of anti-government "militia" movements, partly in response to tragic incidents at Ruby Ridge, Idaho in 1992, and the Branch Davidian siege in Waco, Texas in 1993, prompted fears of radical right-wing violence. These fears were magnified after the April 1995 destruction of the Alfred P. Murrah Federal Building in Oklahoma City, one of the deadliest acts of domestic terrorism in American history.

In the wake of the Oklahoma City bombing, both the House and Senate Judiciary Committees conducted hearings into the threat posed by right-wing domestic terrorists or by elements of the militia movement. On April 27, 1995, a mere eight days after the Oklahoma City bombing, the Senate Judiciary Committee held a hearing looking at "Terrorism in the United States." Among the witnesses who testified were several top law enforcement officials, including FBI Director Louis J. Freeh.

Less than two months later, on June 15, 1995, the Senate Judiciary Committee's Subcommittee on Terrorism, Technology, and Government Information held a hearing on "The Militia Movement in the United States." Once again, a number of federal, state, and local law enforcement officials testified about threats and acts of violence by people tied to militia groups. However, this hearing also featured testimony by five individuals affiliated with various militia groups. Not surprisingly, they denied any involvement in the Oklahoma

The remains of the Alfred P. Murrah Federal Building, Oklahoma City, OK, April 19, 1995. The bombing, which claimed the lives of 168 people, prompted a wave of concern over the "militia movement" and other right-wing extremists. Source: https://www.fbi.gov/history/famous-cases/oklahoma-city-bombing

City attack or other acts of terrorism, as well as any ties to neo-Nazis or white supremacists.

Finally, on November 2, 1995, the House Judiciary Committee's Sub-committee on Crime held a hearing on the "Nature and Threat of Violent Anti-Government Groups in America." It is unlikely that these hearings impacted the militia movement and radical right in the same way that the HUAC hearings affected the UKA. They did, however, serve as part of a broader attempt to focus official and public concern on armed right-wing bodies. This campaign of publicity, in the wake of the Oklahoma City atrocity, undoubtedly contributed a great deal to the decline of the militia movement and radical right in the late 1990s.

Congress and the Alt-Right: 2019–Present

With the rise of white nationalism and the alt-right in recent years, congressional committees have once again inquired into the nature and activities of right-wing radicals. These investigations have been given further impetus by the violent plots against public officials resulting from COVID-19 restrictions, and of course, the January 6th assault on the Capitol. Between 2019–22, Congress held approximately 20 hearings dealing with the topics of domestic terrorism and right-wing extremism, not including the work of the January 6th Committee. These hearing transcripts offer a wealth of information on these movements, while also often reflecting the partisan polarization and divisions that have facilitated their rise. A lengthy, but not exhaustive, list of these hearings follows below.

Congressional Hearings on the KKK and the Militia Movement

Activities of Ku Klux Klan Organizations in the United States. Hearings Before the Committee on Un-American Activities, House of Representatives, Eighty-Ninth Congress, First (-Second) Session. 1965–66, 5 pts. + index

The Militia Movement in the United States. Hearing Before the Subcommittee on Terrorism, Technology, and Government Information of the Committee on the Judiciary, United States Senate, One Hundred Fourth Congress, First Session. 1997.

Nature and Threat of Violent Anti-Government Groups in America. Hearing Before the Subcommittee on Crime of the Committee on the Judiciary, House of Representatives, One Hundred Fourth Congress, First Session. 1996.

The Present-Day Ku Klux Klan Movement. Report by the Committee on Un-American Activities, House of Representatives, Ninetieth Congress, First Session. December 11, 1967.

Terrorism in the United States: The Nature and Extent of the Threat and Possible Legislative Responses. Hearing Before the Committee on the Judiciary, United States Senate, One Hundred Fourth Congress, First Session. 1997.

Congressional Committee Hearings on Right-Wing Extremism: 2019–22

Assessing the Threat from Accelerationists and Militia Extremists: Hearing Before the Subcommittee on Intelligence and Counterterrorism of the Committee on Homeland Security, House of Representatives, One Hundred Sixteenth Congress, Second Session, July 16, 2020. https://purl.fdlp.gov/GPO/gpo153852.

Confronting the Rise of Domestic Terrorism in the Homeland: Hearing Before the Committee on Homeland Security, House of Representatives, One Hundred Sixteenth Congress, First Session. May 8, 2019. https://purl.fdlp.gov/GPO/gpo127521.

Confronting Violent White Supremacy (Part III): Addressing the Transnational Terrorist Threat. *Joint Hearing Before the Subcommittee on National Security and the Subcommittee on Civil Rights and Civil Liberties of the Committee on Oversight and Reform, House of Representatives, One Hundred Sixteenth Congress, First Session.* September 20, 2019. https://purl.fdlp.gov/GPO/gpo123245.

Confronting White Supremacy (Part I): The Consequences of Inaction. Hearing Before the Subcommittee on Civil Rights and Civil Liberties of the Committee on Oversight and Reform, House of Representatives, One Hundred Sixteenth Congress, First Session. May 15, 2019. https://purl.fdlp.gov/GPO/gpo123245.

Confronting White Supremacy (Part II): Adequacy of the Federal Response. Hearing Before the Subcommittee on Civil Rights and Civil Liberties of the Committee on Oversight and Reform, House of Representatives, One Hundred Sixteenth Congress, First Session. June 4, 2019. https://purl.fdlp.gov/GPO/gpo123245.

Countering Domestic Terrorism: Examining the Evolving Threat. Hearing Before the Committee on Homeland Security and Governmental Affairs, United States

Senate, One Hundred Sixteenth Congress, First Session. September 25, 2019. https://purl.fdlp.gov/GPO/gpo133354.

Domestic Violent Extremism in America: Hearing Before the Committee on Appropriations, United States Senate, One Hundred Seventeenth Congress, First Session: Special Hearing, May 12, 2021, Washington, DC. https://purl.fdlp.gov/GPO/gpo189546.

The Dynamic Terrorism Landscape and What it Means for America: Hearing Before the Committee on Homeland Security, House of Representatives, One Hundred Seventeenth Congress, Second Session. February 2, 2022. https://purl.fdlp.gov/GPO/gpo177735.

Examining the Domestic Terrorism Threat in the Wake of the Attack on the U.S. Capitol: Hearing Before the Committee on Homeland Security, House of Representatives, One Hundred Seventeenth Congress, First Session. February 4, 2021. https://purl.fdlp.gov/GPO/gpo154925.

Hate Crimes and the Rise of White Nationalism. Hearing Before the Committee on the Judiciary, House of Representatives, One Hundred Sixteenth Congress, First Session. April 9, 2019. https://purl.fdlp.gov/GPO/gpo157979.

Meeting the Challenge of White Nationalist Terrorism at Home and Abroad. Joint Hearing Before the Subcommittee on the Middle East, North Africa, and International Terrorism of the Committee on Foreign Affairs, with the Subcommittee on Intelligence and Counterterrorism of the Committee on Homeland Security, House of Representatives, One Hundred Sixteenth Congress, First Session. September 18, 2019. http://purl.fdlp.gov/GPO/gpo130111.

Racially and Ethnically Motivated Violent Extremism: The Transnational Threat: Hearing Before the Subcommittee on Intelligence and Counterterrorism of the Committee on Homeland Security, House of Representatives, One Hundred Seventeenth Congress, First Session. April 29, 2021. https://purl.fdlp.gov/GPO/gpo157104.

The Rise in Violence Against Minority Institutions: Hearing Before the Subcommittee on Crime, Terrorism, and Homeland Security of the Committee on the Judiciary, U.S. House of Representatives, One Hundred Seventeenth Congress, Second Session. February 17, 2022. https://purl.fdlp.gov/GPO/gpo188222.

The Rise of Domestic Terrorism in America: Hearing Before the Subcommittee on Crime, Terrorism, and Homeland Security of the Committee on the Judiciary, U.S. House of Representatives, One Hundred Seventeenth Congress, First Session. Wednesday, February 24, 2021. https://purl.fdlp.gov/GPO/gpo174912.

Social Media Platforms and the Amplification of Domestic Extremism and Other Harmful Content: Hearing Before the Committee on Homeland Security and

Governmental Affairs, United States Senate, One Hundred Seventeenth Congress, First Session. October 28, 2021. https://purl.fdlp.gov/GPO /gpo190147.

State and Local Responses to Domestic Terrorism: The Attack on the U.S. Capitol and Beyond: Hearing Before the Subcommittee on Intelligence and Counterterrorism of the Committee on Homeland Security, House of Representatives, One Hundred Seventeenth Congress, First Session. March 24, 2021. https://purl.fdlp.gov/GPO/gpo155904.

Additional Sources

Belew, Kathleen. *Bring the War Home: The White Power Movement and Paramilitary America.* Cambridge, MA: Harvard University Press, 2018.

Churchill, Robert H. *To Shake Their Guns in the Tyrant's Face: Libertarian Political Violence and the Origins of the Militia Movement.* Ann Arbor: University of Michigan Press, 2009.

Cunningham, David. Klansville, U.S.A. *The Rise and Fall of the Civil Rights-Era Ku Klux Klan.* New York: Oxford University Press, 2013.

Hawley, George. *Making Sense of the Alt-Right.* New York: Columbia University Press, 2017.

Neiwert, David. *Alt-America: The Rise of the Radical Right in the Age of Trump.* London: Verso, 2017.

Wade, Wyn Craig. *The Fiery Cross: The Ku Klux Klan in America.* New York: Simon and Schuster, 1987.

2

1983

The Bombing of the U.S. Capitol

AS MANY HAVE NOTED, the January 6th, 2021 storming of the U.S. Capitol by a violent right-wing mob was the first successful seizure of the structure since it was taken by the British in 1814. However, it was not the first time that domestic extremists had targeted the capitol building. In 1954, armed Puerto Rican nationalists wounded five members of Congress in a shooting spree. In 1971, the radical left Weather Underground detonated a bomb in a north wing restroom that caused minor damage. Most recently, in 1983, a Marxist-Leninist terrorist group exploded a bomb that caused extensive damage to the Senate side of the building. This incident, though now largely forgotten, was arguably the most destructive domestic terror attack on the U.S. Capitol prior to January 6.

The Bombing

On the night of November 7, 1983, just moments after a phone warning was received, a bomb detonated on the second floor of the north (Senate) wing of the capitol. An article on the Senate history website describes the damage:

> The force of the device, hidden under a bench at the eastern end of the corridor outside the chamber, blew off the door to the office of Democratic Leader Robert C. Byrd. The blast also punched a potentially lethal hole in a wall partition sending a shower of pulverized brick, plaster, and glass into the Republican cloakroom. Although the explosion caused no structural damage to the Capitol, it shattered mirrors, chandeliers, and furniture. Officials calculated damages of $250,000. ("Bomb Explodes in Capitol")

Aftermath of the November 7, 1983 bombing of the U.S. Capitol building. Source: Wikimedia Commons via Smithsonian Magazine: https://www.smithsonianmag .com/smart-news/history-violent-attacks-capitol-180976704/.

There were no casualties. The bombing was claimed by the "Armed Resistance Unit," as a response to recent American military interventions in Grenada and Lebanon. The name "Armed Resistance Unit," investigation would reveal, was a cover adopted by a group whose real name was the May 19th Communist Organization.

The May 19th Communist Organization

In 1978, a radical Marxist-Leninist faction split off from the Weather Underground to form their own group. They called themselves the May 19th

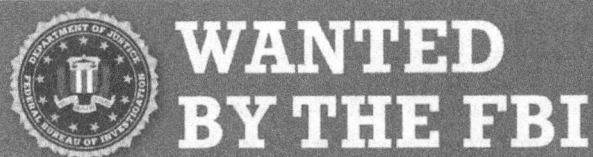

ELIZABETH ANNA DUKE

Unlawful Possession of United States Identification; Conspiracy; Unlawful Storage of Explosives; Unlawful Possession of Firearms and Destructive Devices; Storage and Concealment of Stolen Explosives; Unlawful Possession of Five or More False Identification Documents; Possession of Counterfeit Social Security Cards; Aiding and Abetting; Unlawful Possession of Document-Making Implement

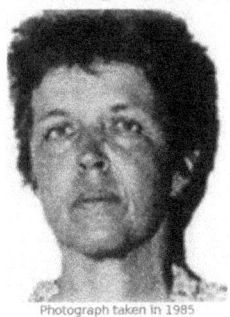

Photograph taken in 1985

Current FBI wanted poster for Elizabeth Anna Duke, a fugitive member of the May 19th Communist Organization. Source: https://www.fbi.gov/wanted /dt/elizabeth-anna-duke.

Communist Organization, in honor of the mutual birthday of Malcolm X and North Vietnamese communist leader Ho Chi Minh. While the May 19th organization was largely white, it did ally itself with radical Black and Puerto Rican groups, even aiding in two 1979 prison escapes. One unique aspect of the group was that it was mostly founded and led by women.

Historian William Rosenau describes the May 19th organization as follows:

> They are sort of an offshoot of the Weather Underground, which essentially cracked up in the mid 1980s. These women decided to continue the armed struggle. Many of them had been in the Weather Underground, but they thought the Weather Underground had made important ideological mistakes, that the Weather Underground saw itself as a vanguard of revolution, when in fact the real revolutions were going on

in the third world. Or in the United States itself, in places like Puerto Rico or among Native Americans. (Quoted in Thulin, "In the 1980s")

The capitol bombing was just one of a number of terrorist actions the May 19th organization undertook in order to support Third World revolutionary movements. The group was involved in several armored car robberies, and committed a handful of other bombings in the New York and Washington, D.C. areas. None of the bomb attacks resulted in fatalities, and all followed the same basic script. In Rosenau's words: "a warning call to clear the area, an explosion, a pre-recorded message to media railing against U.S. imperialism or the war machine under various organizational aliases (never using the name M19)." (Quoted in ibid.)

In the wake of the U.S. Capitol bombing, the group became a major target of FBI counterterrorism efforts. Even as May 19th became ever more radicalized, contemplating both targeted assassinations and no-warning bombings, the group began to break apart under FBI pressure. The first members were arrested in 1985. In 1988, six members of May 19th were charged with the U.S. Capitol attack as well as several other bombings. Three were convicted in 1990.

While the May 19th Communist Organization largely ceased to exist in the mid-1980s, several members remain at-large, and are sought by the FBI to this day.

Primary Sources

Current and Proposed Security Relating to the U.S. Capitol Building and Grounds: Master Plan for the U.S. Capitol Grounds and Related Areas. Subcommittee on Public Buildings and Grounds of the Committee on Public Works and Transportation, House of Representatives, Ninety-Eighth Congress, First Session. November 15, 1983.

Domestic Security Measures Relating to Terrorism. Hearings Before the Subcommittee on Civil and Constitutional Rights of the Committee on the Judiciary, House of Representatives, Ninety-Eighth Congress, Second Session. 1984.

FBI Oversight and Budget Authorization. Hearing Before the Subcommittee on Security and Terrorism of the Committee on the Judiciary, United States Senate, Ninety-Eighth Congress, Second Session. March 14, 1984.

FBI Oversight and Budget Authorization for Fiscal Year 1986. Hearing Before the Subcommittee on Security and Terrorism of the Committee on the Judiciary, United States Senate, Ninety-Ninth Congress, First Session. April 3, 1985.

The Weather Underground. Report by the Subcommittee to Investigate the Administration of the Internal Security Act and Other Internal Security Laws of the Committee on the Judiciary, United States Senate, Ninety-Fourth Congress, First Session. January 1975.

Additional Sources

"Bomb Explodes in Capitol: November 7, 1983." United States Senate Website. (Available via Internet Archive) https://web.archive.org/web/20220114011256 /https:/www.senate.gov/artandhistory/history/minute/bomb_explodes_in _capitol.htm.

McGreevy, Nora. "The History of Violent Attacks on the U.S. Capitol." Smithsonianmag.com, January 8, 2021. https://www.smithsonianmag.com /smart-news/history-violent-attacks-capitol-180976704/.

Rosenau, William. *Tonight We Bombed the U.S. Capitol: The Explosive Story of M19, America's First Female Terrorist Group.* New York: Atria Books, 2019.

Thulin, Lila. "In the 1980s, a Far-Left, Female-Led Domestic Terrorism Group Bombed the U.S. Capitol." Smithsonianmag.com, January 6, 2020. https://www.smithsonianmag.com/history/1980s-far-left-female-led -domestic-terrorism-group-bombed-us-capitol-180973904/.

3

Russian Interference in the 2016 Election

Official Russian passport of Aleksei Sergeyevich Morenets, a GRU officer with Unit 26165. Released by the Department of Justice as an exhibit accompanying the indictment of Morenets and six of his colleagues, October 4, 2018. Source: https://www.justice.gov/opa/documents -and-resources-october-4-2018-press-conference

Part 1: Fancy Bear and the GRU

It has been widely reported that the 2016 election-related hacking of email accounts affiliated with the Democratic Party and Hillary Clinton campaign was the work of hackers affiliated with Russian military intelligence, the Glavnoye Razvedyvatel'noye Upravlenie (GRU), the Main Intelligence Directorate of the Armed Forces General Staff. Known as Advanced Persistent Threat (APT) 28, or "Fancy Bear," among other terms, the GRU hacking unit has been one of the world's most active. A number of recent documents released by the US Department of Justice and several allied governments have provided much greater detail on the GRU's cyber activities.

Unit 26165

A July 13, 2018 indictment returned by a grand jury in the District of Columbia revealed that "Fancy Bear" is, in fact, part of the GRU. Known officially as Unit 26165, the section consists of Russian military intelligence officers trained in hacking and cyberespionage. Beginning in March 2016, Unit 26165 began targeting individuals affiliated with the Clinton campaign and Democratic Party:

> In 2016, officials in Unit 26165 began spearphishing volunteers and employees of the presidential campaign of Hillary Clinton, including the campaign's chairman. Through that process, officials in this unit were able to steal the usernames and passwords for numerous individuals and use those credentials to steal email content and hack into other computers. They also were able to hack into the computer networks of the Democratic Congressional Campaign Committee (DCCC) and the Democratic National Committee (DNC) through these spearphishing techniques to steal emails and documents, covertly monitor the computer activity of dozens of employees, and implant hundreds of files of malicious computer code to steal passwords and maintain access to these networks. ("Grand Jury Indicts 12 Russian Intelligence Officers")

According to the indictment, over 300 persons were targeted by Unit 26165 as part of their election-related hacking.

The stolen information was then weaponized as part of what is termed an "active measures" campaign, beginning in June 2016. This part of the operation, which involved releasing the various documents obtained in order to shape public opinion, was conducted by a separate GRU cyber element called Unit 74455. This unit created a website called DC Leaks, as well as a fake online persona called "Guccifer 2.0", an alleged Romanian hacker who claimed credit for the DNC hack. In July, Guccifer 2.0 passed on the stolen material to WikiLeaks, who began releasing it later that month.

In all, 12 GRU officers were indicted on July 13. Nine of them were members of Unit 26165, including its commanding officer, Viktor Borisovich Netyksho. The other three were members of Unit 74455, including its commander, Colonel Aleksandr Vladimirovich Osadchuk.

Other GRU Hacking Operations

The broader scope of Unit 26165's hacking was revealed by a second American indictment, this one from a grand jury in the Western District of Pennsylvania, and released on October 4, 2018. This indictment charged seven GRU officers with "computer hacking, wire fraud, aggravated identity theft, and money laundering." Five of the seven men indicted were identified as part of Unit 26165, and three of those five had already been indicted in July for election-related hacking:

> According to the indictment, beginning in or around December 2014 and continuing until at least May 2018, the conspiracy conducted persistent and sophisticated computer intrusions affecting U.S. persons, corporate entities, international organizations, and their respective employees located around the world, based on their strategic interest to the Russian government.
>
> Among the goals of the conspiracy was to publicize stolen information as part of an influence and disinformation campaign designed to undermine, retaliate against, and otherwise delegitimize the efforts of international anti-doping organizations and officials who had publicly exposed a Russian state-sponsored athlete doping program and to damage the reputations of athletes around the world by falsely claiming that such athletes were using banned or performance-enhancing drugs. ("U.S. Charges Russian GRU Officers")

Among the specific targets of these GRU cyberespionage efforts were: the World Anti-Doping Agency; the United States Anti-Doping Agency; The Organisation for the Prohibition of Chemical Weapons; and Westinghouse

Electric Company. The international scope of the GRU's efforts is corroborated by additional information released on October 4 in support of the US indictment, by the United Kingdom, Netherlands, and Canada.

Primary Sources on Unit 26165

"Documents and Resources from the October 4, 2018 Press Conference." Department of Justice Office of Public Affairs, October 4, 2018. https://www .justice.gov/opa/documents-and-resources-october-4-2018-press-conference.
"Grand Jury Indicts 12 Russian Intelligence Officers for Hacking Offenses Related to the 2016 Election." Department of Justice Office of Public Affairs, July 13, 2018. https://www.justice.gov/opa/pr/grand-jury-indicts-12-russian-intelligence -officers-hacking-offenses-related-2016-election.
National Security Archive. "Cyber Brief: GRU Cyber Operations." https://nsarchive .gwu.edu/news/cyber-vault/2018-07-18/cyber-brief-gru-cyber-operations.
"Netherlands Defence Intelligence and Security Service Disrupts Russian Cyber Operation Targeting OPCW." Netherlands Ministry of Defence, October 4, 2018. https://www.asdnews.com/news/defense/2018/10/04/netherlands -defence-intelligence-security-service-disrupts-russian-cyber-operation -targeting-opcw.
"Reckless Campaign of Cyber Attacks by Russian Military intelligence Service Exposed." UK National Cyber Security Centre, October 4, 2018. https://www .ncsc.gov.uk/news/reckless-campaign-cyber-attacks-russian-military -intelligence-service-exposed.
"U.S. Charges Russian GRU Officers with International Hacking and Related Influence and Disinformation Operations." Department of Justice Office of Public Affairs, October 4, 2018. https://www.justice.gov/opa/pr/us-charges -russian-gru-officers-international-hacking-and-related-influence-and.
U.S. v. Aleksei Sergeyevich Morenets, et al. Department of Justice, October 4, 2018. https://www.justice.gov/opa/page/file/1098481/download.
U.S. v. Viktor Borisovich Netyksho, et al. Department of Justice, July 13, 2018. https://www.justice.gov/file/1080281/download.

Part 2: "Putin's Chef" and the "Troll Farm": Russian Social Media Subversion in 2016

Much of the discussion around Russia's interference in the 2016 US presidential election has focused on the manipulation of social media through the use of "bots" and "trolls" to shape American views and online discourse. As

Image shared on social media in 2016 by Russian troll account called "Army of Jesus." Released by the Senate Intelligence Committee, November 1, 2017. Source: https://twitter.com/MarkWarner/status/925802644869959680

Attorney General William P. Barr put it in his March 24, 2019 letter to key congressional leaders, this effort:

> involved attempts by a Russian organization, the Internet Research Agency (IRA), to conduct disinformation and social media operations in the United States designed to sow social discord, eventually with the aim of interfering with the election. (Barr, "AG March 24 2019 Letter," 2)

Building housing the Internet Research Agency, St. Petersburg, Russia.
Source: Radio Free Europe/Radio Liberty: https://www.rferl.org/a/us
-russia-facebook-manipulation-echoes-troll-factory-accounts/28722595.html

Even prior to the release of Special Counsel Robert Mueller's report, it is important to note that previous legal filings and congressional documents already revealed a great deal about the Russian 2016 social media campaign.

"Putin's Chef": Yevgeniy Prigozhin and the Internet Research Agency:

Unlike the much-publicized 2016 hacking of email accounts affiliated with the Democratic party and Hillary Clinton campaign, which was carried out by Russia's military intelligence service, the GRU, Russia's social media disinformation campaign was not the work of an official Russian state agency. Rather, it was a private agency, owned by a Russian oligarch, that unleashed bots and trolls across Twitter, Facebook, Instagram, and other social media platforms in order to impact how Americans voted in 2016.

Dubbed the "troll farm", the Internet Research Agency (IRA), based in St. Petersburg, Russia, was established as a legal corporate entity around July

2013. A February 2018 US Department of Justice press release summarizes the IRA's activities:

> Internet Research Agency allegedly operated through Russian shell companies. It employed hundreds of persons for its online operations, ranging from creators of fictitious personas to technical and administrative support, with an annual budget of millions of dollars. Internet Research Agency was a structured organization headed by a management group and arranged in departments, including graphics, search-engine optimization, information technology, and finance departments. ("Grand Jury Indicts")

The driving force behind the IRA is a St. Petersburg-based Russian oligarch named Yevgeniy Prigozhin. Starting as a restaurant owner, Prigozhin has expanded his operations to the point where he holds a number of large Russian government catering contracts, earning him the nickname "Putin's Chef". He is also now infamous for owning and operating PMC Wagner, a private military contractor whose mercenaries have come to play a major role in Russian military operations in Ukraine.

Project Lakhta and the 2016 US Presidential Election

In 2014, the IRA became part of a broader Prigozhin-financed initiative called Project Lakhta. The purpose of Project Lakhta is to use the Internet and social media to help shape public opinion both inside and outside Russia in accord with the interests of the Russian Federation. These efforts were soon expanded to include the United States. By April 2014, a unit was formed within the IRA called the "translator project", that concentrated its efforts on American public opinion. According to a February 2018 indictment by the Department of Justice, the translator project "focused on the U.S. population and conducted operations on social media platforms such as YouTube, Facebook, Instagram, and Twitter." (United States of America v. Internet Research Agency, 6) In its own words, the IRA existed in part to conduct "information warfare against the United States of America." (ibid.) By July 2016, over 80 IRA employees were assigned to the translator project.

The employees working in the translator project soon created an extensive number of fake social media accounts, claiming to represent both individuals and organizations. They quickly ramped up their activities in an explicit attempt to influence American public opinion during the 2016 presidential election. These efforts are described in detail in a February 2018 Department of Justice press release:

> To hide the Russian origin of their activities, the defendants allegedly purchased space on computer servers located within the United States in order to set up a virtual private network. The defendants allegedly used that infrastructure to establish hundreds of accounts on social media networks such as Facebook, Instagram, and Twitter, making it appear that the accounts were controlled by persons within the United States. They used stolen or fictitious American identities, fraudulent bank accounts, and false identification documents. The defendants posed as politically and socially active Americans, advocating for and against particular political candidates. They established social media pages and groups to communicate with unwitting Americans. They also purchased political advertisements on social media. ("Grand Jury Indicts")

Prigozhin was the primary source of funding for the IRA and the other elements of Project Lakhta. From January 2016 to June 2018, the total proposed budget for Project Lakhta was around $35,000,000 (for all operations, not just those targeted at the US). Over $10,000,000 were budgeted for Project Lakhta in the first half of 2018 alone. A St. Petersburg accountant named Elena Khusyaynova oversaw Project Lakhta's budget.

The Extent and Impact of the IRA's Activity

Just how extensive, and how effective, were the efforts of Project Lakhta in swaying American voters? While the latter question remains very much in dispute, recent research has revealed that the IRA's efforts to influence the US public were far wider in scope than first believed. In particular, a pair of reports prepared at the request of the Senate Select Committee on Intelligence and released in December 2018, have revealed that IRA-created social media content reached tens of millions of Americans between 2014–2017.

According to the first of these reports, from the Computational Propaganda Research Project at the University of Oxford, posts created for IRA-run Facebook accounts were "shared by users just under 31 million times, liked almost 39 million times, reacted to with emojis almost 5.4 million times, and engaged sufficient users to generate almost 3.5 million comments." (Howard et al., "The IRA, Social Media," 6) The 20 most popular IRA Facebook pages received 99% of this usage.

IRA-created Instagram accounts directed at Americans were likewise heavily used. IRA-created Instagram posts "garnered almost 185 million likes and users commented about 4 million times. Forty pages received 99% of all likes." (Ibid., 7) In all, according to the Oxford researchers, "Over 30 million users, between 2015 and 2017, shared the IRA's Facebook and Instagram posts with their friends and family, liking, reacting to, and commenting on them along the way." (Ibid., 3)

According to the second report, produced by a company called New Knowledge, there were 3,841 fake Twitter accounts run by the IRA, which produced some 6,000,000 tweets, leading to 73,000,000 user engagements via that platform.

Both reports note that the IRA's content was targeted at a number of very specific American demographics from across the political spectrum: African-Americans; conservatives; liberals, especially the LGBT community; Latinos, and Muslim-Americans. While the specific messages tailored to each group varied, all carried a common underlying theme of seeking to exacerbate divisions in American society. In the words of the New Knowledge authors:

> The themes selected by the IRA were deployed to create and reinforce tribalism within each targeted community; in a majority of the posts created on a given Page or account, the IRA simply reinforced in-group camaraderie. They punctuated cultural-affinity content with political posts, and content demonizing out-groups. (DiResta et al., "Tactics & Tropes," 12)

A second major theme both reports agree on is that the IRA's efforts were clearly intended to help elect Donald Trump. To quote the Oxford report:

> What is clear is that all of the messaging clearly sought to benefit the Republican Party—and specifically, Donald Trump. Trump is mentioned most in campaigns targeting conservatives and right-wing voters, where the messaging encouraged these groups to support his campaign. The main groups that could challenge Trump were then provided messaging that sought to confuse, distract, and ultimately discourage members from voting. While the IRA strategy was a long-term one, it is clear that activity between 2015 and 2016 was designed to benefit President Trump's campaign.

(Howard et al., "The IRA, Social Media," 18)

Not content with seeking to influence the outcome of the 2016 US elections, the Russian social media campaign actually intensified following the vote. IRA usage of Facebook and especially Instagram increased in late 2016–2017. Following on the perceived success of the IRA's efforts, it is highly likely that Russia and other foreign actors will seek to use social media to manipulate American opinion in future.

Federal Government Sources on the Internet Research Agency:

Barr, William P. "AG March 24 2019 Letter to House and Senate Judiciary Committees." Committee on the Judiciary, US House of Representatives March 24, 2019. (Available via Internet Archive) https://archive.org /details/5779711-AG-March-24-2019-Letter-to-House-and-Senate.

DiResta, Renee, Kris Shaffer, Becky Ruppel, David Sullivan, Robert Matney, Ryan Fox, Jonathan Albright and Ben Johnson. "The Tactics & Tropes of the Internet Research Agency." New Knowledge, 2018. https://digitalcommons .unl.edu/senatedocs/2/.

"Grand Jury Indicts Thirteen Russian Individuals and Three Russian Companies for Scheme to Interfere in the United States Political System." Department of Justice Office of Public Affairs, February 16, 2018. https://www.justice.gov/opa /pr/grand-jury-indicts-thirteen-russian-individuals-and-three-russian -companies-scheme-interfere.

Howard, Philip N., Bharath Ganesh, Dimitra Liotsiou, John Kelly & Camille François. "The IRA, Social Media and Political Polarization in the United States, 2012–2018." Working Paper 2018.2. Oxford, UK: Project on Computational Propaganda. https://demtech.oii.ox.ac.uk/wp-content/uploads /sites/12/2018/12/The-IRA-Social-Media-and-Political-Polarization.pdf.

Open Hearing on Foreign Influence Operations' Use of Social Media Platforms (Company Witnesses): Hearing Before the Select Committee on Intelligence of the United States Senate, One Hundred Fifteenth Congress, Second Session. September 5, 2018. https://purl.fdlp.gov/GPO/gpo116516.

Open Hearing on Foreign Influence Operations' Use of Social Media Platforms (Third Party Expert Witnesses): Hearing Before the Select Committee on Intelligence of the United States Senate, One Hundred Fifteenth Congress, Second Session. August 1, 2018. https://purl.fdlp.gov/GPO/gpo113350.

Open Hearing: Social Media Influence in the 2016 U.S. Election: Hearing Before the Select Committee on Intelligence of the United States Senate, One Hundred

Fifteenth Congress, First Session. November 1, 2017. https://purl.fdlp.gov/GPO
/gpo93340.

*Report of the House Permanent Select Committee on Intelligence on Russian Active
Measures, Together with Minority Views.* December 31, 2018. https://purl.fdlp
.gov/GPO/gpo114379.

"Russian National Charged with Interfering in U.S. Political System."
Department of Justice Office of Public Affairs, October 19, 2018. https://www
.justice.gov/opa/pr/russian-national-charged-interfering-us-political-system.

"Social Media Influence in the 2016 U.S. Elections Exhibits." Senate Select
Committee on Intelligence, November 1, 2017. https://www.intelligence
.senate.gov/hearings/open-hearing-social-media-influence-2016-us-elections.

United States of America v. Elena Alekseevna Khusyaynova. Department of
Justice, September 28, 2018. https://www.justice.gov/opa/press-release/file
/1102316/download.

United States of America v. Internet Research Agency LLC [and 15 others],
Defendants: Case 1:18-cr-00032-DLF. United States District Court for the
District of Columbia, February 16, 2018. http://purl.fdlp.gov/GPO/gpo89499.

Additional Sources on the Internet Research
Agency and the 2016 Elections

Gadde, Vijaya and Yoel Roth. "Enabling Further Research of Information
Operations on Twitter." Twitter.com, October 17, 2018. https://blog.twitter
.com/official/en_us/topics/company/2018/enabling-further-research-of
-information-operations-on-twitter.html.

"Itemized Posts and Historical Engagement – 6 Now-Closed FB Pages."
https://public.tableau.com/profile/d1gi#!/vizhome/FB4/TotalReachbyPage.

Roeder, Oliver. "Why We're Sharing 3 Million Russian Troll Tweets."
FiveThirtyEight.com, July 31, 2018.https://fivethirtyeight.com/features
/why-were-sharing-3-million-russian-troll-tweets/.

Synovitz, Ron. "Facebook Manipulation Echoes Accounts From Russian 'Troll
Factory'." Radio Free Europe/Radio Liberty, September 7 2017.
https://www.rferl.org/a/us-russia-facebook-manipulation-echoes-troll
-factory-accounts/28722595.html.

"#TrollTracker: Twitter Troll Farm Archives." Digital Forensic Research Lab,
Atlantic Council, October 17, 2018. https://medium.com/dfrlab
/trolltracker-twitter-troll-farm-archives-8d5dd61c486b.

4

Foreign Election Influence in 2020

I N THE LATE SUMMER AND FALL OF 2020, the U. S. government issued a number of warnings about attempts by foreign governments to influence the upcoming American presidential election, with officials indicating that Russia, China, and Iran posed the main threats. In Spring 2021, the U.S. Intelligence Community (IC) has provided further information on the nature and extent of foreign election influence operations in 2020, information that has permitted us to revise and update the picture presented last fall.

Election Influence Versus Election Interference:

In its analyses, the U.S. IC distinguishes between election influence and election interference. From a March 2021 assessment:

Election influence includes overt and covert efforts by foreign governments or actors acting as agents of, or on behalf of, foreign governments intended to affect directly or indirectly a US election – including candidates, political parties, voters or their preferences, or political processes. **Election interference** is a subset of election influence activities targeted at the technical aspects of the election, including voter registration, casting and counting ballots, or reporting results (*Intelligence Community Assessment*, 1; bold in original)

In short, election influence involves efforts to impact the opinions and preferences of voters, parties, and candidates. Election interference involves trying to alter the processes and infrastructure of an election, including vote tallies.

After analyzing the evidence the US IC found no evidence of foreign election interference in 2020. In the words of a March 16, 2021 joint statement from the Departments of Justice and Homeland Security, while "Russian, Chinese, and Iranian government-affiliated actors materially impacted the security of certain networks during the 2020 federal elections, the Departments found no evidence that any foreign government-affiliated actor manipulated election results or otherwise compromised the integrity of the 2020 federal elections." ("Joint Statement from the Departments")

Foreign government efforts at election influence, however, were another matter.

Three Main Threats: Russia, China, and Iran

The most thorough official overview of the influence threat posed to the 2020 election by foreign actors came in an August 7 statement by William Evanina, Director of the National Counterintelligence and Security Center (NCSC). Evanina stated that:

> Foreign states will continue to use covert and overt influence measures in their attempts to sway U.S. voters' preferences and perspectives, shift U.S. policies, increase discord in the United States, and undermine the American people's confidence in our democratic process. ("Statement by NCSC Director")

Evanina announced that the three main adversaries seeking to achieve these ends were China, Russia, and Iran:

> We assess that China prefers that President Trump – whom Beijing sees as unpredictable – does not win reelection. China has been expanding its influence efforts ahead of November 2020 to shape the policy environment in the United States, pressure political figures it views as opposed to China's interests, and deflect and counter criticism of China.
>
> We assess that Russia is using a range of measures to primarily denigrate former Vice President Biden and what it sees as an anti-Russia "establishment." This is consistent with Moscow's public criticism of him when he was Vice President for his role in the Obama Administration's policies on Ukraine and its support for the anti-Putin opposition inside Russia....Some Kremlin-linked actors are also seeking to boost President Trump's candidacy on social media and Russian television.

We assess that Iran seeks to undermine U.S. democratic institutions, President Trump, and to divide the country in advance of the 2020 elections. ("Statement by NCSC Director")

Microsoft Warns About "Strontium," Zirconium," and "Phosphorus"

In a September 10, 2020 blog post, Microsoft executive Tom Burt stated that three major cyber threat organizations, linked to each of the three nation-states mentioned by Evanina, had been detected:

> Strontium, operating from Russia, has attacked more than 200 organizations including political campaigns, advocacy groups, parties and political consultants
>
> Zirconium, operating from China, has attacked high-profile individuals associated with the election, including people associated with the Joe Biden for President campaign and prominent leaders in the international affairs community
>
> Phosphorus, operating from Iran, has continued to attack the personal accounts of people associated with the Donald J. Trump for President campaign ("New Cyberattacks")

Burt reported that "Microsoft's Threat Intelligence Center (MSTIC) has observed a series of attacks conducted by Strontium between September 2019 and today," in order to "harvest people's log-in credentials or compromise their accounts, presumably to aid in intelligence gathering or disruption operations." According to Burt, Strontium is the same body "identified in the Mueller report as the organization primary responsible for the attacks on the Democratic presidential campaign in 2016." This would mean that Strontium is, in fact, Unit 26165 of the GRU, Russian military intelligence. Unit 26165 was also identified as the GRU's 85th Main Special Service Center in an August 13 NSA/FBI joint press release.

Sanctioning Russian Disinformation Outlets

Also on September 10, the same day Microsoft released its warning of foreign cyber interference, the Treasury Department announced sanctions against a pro-Russian Ukrainian lawmaker, Andrii Derkach, for actively seeking to influence the 2020 U. S. presidential election. Treasury described Derkach as "an active Russian agent for over a decade, maintaining close connections with the Russian Intelligence Services." The press release announcing the sanctions discussed his activities as follows:

> From at least late 2019 through mid-2020, Derkach waged a covert influence campaign centered on cultivating false and unsubstantiated narratives concerning U.S. officials in the upcoming 2020 Presidential Election, spurring corruption investigations in both Ukraine and the United States designed to culminate prior to election day. Derkach's unsubstantiated narratives were pushed in Western media through coverage of press conferences and other news events, including interviews and statements.
>
> Between May and July 2020, Derkach released edited audio tapes and other unsupported information with the intent to discredit U.S. officials, and he levied unsubstantiated allegations against U.S. and international political figures. Derkach almost certainly targeted the U.S. voting populace, prominent U.S. persons, and members of the U.S. government, based on his reliance on U.S. platforms, English-language documents and videos, and pro-Russian lobbyists in the United States used to propagate his claims. ("Treasury Sanctions Russia-Linked")

According to media reports, Derkach's efforts were directed against Democratic presidential candidate Joe Biden, and his son Hunter. Among other activities, Derkach has met with President Trump's personal lawyer, Rudolph Giuliani, to discuss alleged wrongdoing by Hunter Biden. Along with Derkach, three employees of Russia's Internet Research Agency, the "troll farm" made notorious by its social media activities in 2016, were likewise sanctioned.

October 2020 Assessment

In October, the Department of Homeland Security released its first ever Homeland Threat Assessment. This document likewise referenced Russia, China, and Iran as the main foreign threats to this November's election. The majority of the election assessment portion was devoted to Russia:

> Russian online influence actors probably will engage in efforts to discourage voter turnout and to suppress votes in the 2020 U.S. election using methods they have deployed since at least 2016. Before the 2016 U.S. Presidential election, Russian trolls directed messages at specific audiences with false information about the time, manner, or place of

voting to suppress votes. Russian influence actors also posed as U.S. persons and discouraged African Americans, Native Americans, and other minority voters from participating in the 2016 election. (*Homeland Threat Assessment*, 12-13)

In contrast with Director Evanina's statement, which emphasized the anti-Biden and pro-Trump nature of much of Russia's efforts, the Homeland Threat Assessment argued that "Moscow's overarching objective is to undermine the U.S. electoral process and weaken the United States through discord, division, and distraction," not to aid or oppose any one candidate. This assessment, if true, would contradict not just the overwhelming intelligence community consensus that Russia sought to aid Donald Trump in 2016, but also the evidence of Andrii Derkach's blatantly anti-Biden efforts and outreach to people around Trump.

Finally, DNI Ratcliffe, in his October 21 statement, noted that "some voter registration information has been obtained by Iran, and separately, by Russia." This information has apparently been used by the Iranians to send threatening emails to some voters, messages labeled as coming from the radical right-wing Proud Boys movement.

Assessing the Impact: Election Influence Efforts by Iran and China

On March 16, 2021 the U.S. Intelligence Community released its overall assessment of foreign efforts to influence the course of the 2020 U.S. elections. Among other conclusions, this document confirmed that Iran was involved in such a campaign:

> We assess with high confidence that Iran carried out an influence campaign during the 2020 US election season intended to undercut the reelection prospects of former President Trump and to further its longstanding objectives of exacerbating divisions in the US, creating confusion, and undermining the legitimacy of US elections and institutions. (*Intelligence Community Assessment*, 5)

As far as China, the IC, in contrast to its fall assessments, stated that "China did not deploy interference efforts and considered but did not deploy influence efforts intended to change the outcome of the US presidential election." This decision by China not to actively seek to influence the election was likely due in part to a Chinese belief that "its traditional influence tools, primarily targeted economic measures and lobbying key individuals and interest groups, would be sufficient to achieve its goal of shaping US policy regardless of who won the election", as well as the fear that the "risk of interference was not worth the reward." (*Intelligence Community Assessment*, 7)

The IC report does note that the National Intelligence Officer for Cyber disagreed with this view, assessing with moderate confidence that the Chinese made some modest efforts to influence the election campaign to Trump's detriment.

Russian Election Influence Efforts

One thing the IC assessment makes abundantly clear is that, just as in 2016, Russia was the major foreign state source of efforts to influence the US election process:

> We assess that President Putin and the Russian state authorized and conducted influence operations against the 2020 US presidential election aimed at denigrating President Biden and the Democratic Party, supporting former President Trump, undermining public confidence in the electoral process, and exacerbating sociopolitical divisions in the US. (*Intelligence Community Assessment*, 2)

Confirming previously released information, the March 16 assessment noted that the Russians utilized influence assets in Ukraine to "launder influence narratives–including misleading or unsubstantiated allegations against President Biden—through US media organizations, US officials, and prominent US individuals, some of whom were close to former President Trump and his administration." (*Intelligence Community Assessment*, 2)

Among the most notable of these conduits was a Ukrainian legislator named Andriy Derkach, who "has ties to Russian officials as well as Russia's intelligence services," and whose activities "Putin had purview over." As noted above, Derkach was already sanctioned by the U.S. Treasury Department last September for his election interference activities, including his infamous meeting with President Trump's personal attorney, Rudolph Giuliani. (Ibid.)

Just as in 2016, the Russian authorities utilized bots, trolls, and other forms of social media activity to spread their preferred U.S. election narratives. Involved in many of these activities was Lakhta Internet Research, the new name for the notorious troll farm formerly known as the Internet Research Agency. According to the March 16 assessment, Russian social media actors also continued their broader attempts to disrupt the cohesion of American society, by promoting "conspiratorial narratives about the COVID-19 pandemic, made allegations of social media censorship, and highlighted US divisions surrounding protests about racial justice." (Ibid., 4)

New Election Influence Sanctions

In response to the extent of Russian efforts to influence the outcome of the 2020 U.S. presidential election, on April 15, 2021 the Treasury Department announced sanctions "against 16 entities and 16 individuals who attempted to influence the 2020 U.S. presidential election at the direction of the leadership of the Russian Government." ("Treasury Escalates Sanctions")

Among the most notable targets of these new sanctions was an individual named Konstantin Kilimnik. The sanctions announcement identified Kilimnik as:

A Russian and Ukrainian political consultant and known Russian Intelligence Services agent implementing influence operations on their behalf. During the 2016 U.S. presidential election campaign, Kilimnik provided the Russian Intelligence Services with sensitive information on polling and campaign strategy. Additionally, Kilimnik sought to promote the narrative that Ukraine, not Russia, had interfered in the 2016 U.S. presidential election. In 2018, Kilimnik was indicted on charges of obstruction of justice and conspiracy to obstruct justice regarding unregistered lobbying work. ("Treasury Escalates Sanctions")

Kilimnik was prominently featured in the Mueller Report due to his close connections with Trump's former campaign manager Paul Manafort. It was the latter who, in 2016, gave Kilimnik the "sensitive information on polling and campaign strategy" that he then gave to Russian intelligence. While the Mueller Report noted that Manafort gave this data to Kilimnik, the April 15 announcement was the first official confirmation that Kilimnik then passed this information on to the Russians. According to media reports, Kilimnik's Russian intelligence ties are primarily with military intelligence, the GRU. (See Bertrand, "The Shadowy Operative") This is the same agency responsible for hacking numerous Democratic Party-related accounts in the spring of 2016, and then releasing the contents to Wikileaks.

The March 16 assessment described Kilimnik as a "Russian influence agent," part of "A network of Ukraine–linked individuals" who in 2020 "took steps throughout the election cycle to damage US ties to Ukraine, denigrate President Biden and his candidacy, and benefit former President Trump's prospects for reelection." (*Intelligence Community Assessment*, 3)

Among other things, the role of Kilimnik shows the essential underlying continuity of Russian efforts at election influence in both 2016 and 2020. In both elections, the goal was to further divide American society, as well as to weaken the Democratic nominee and boost the prospects of Donald Trump.

Federal Government Sources on 2020 Foreign Election Influence

"DNI John Ratcliffe's Remarks at Press Conference on Election Security." Office of the Director of National Intelligence, October 21, 2020. https://www.odni .gov/index.php/newsroom/press-releases/item/2162-dni-john-ratcliffe -s-remarks-at-press-conference-on-election-security.

Intelligence Community Assessment: Foreign Threats to the 2020 U.S. Federal Elections. Office of the Director of National Intelligence, March 16, 2021. https://www.odni.gov/index.php/newsroom/reports-publications/reports -publications-2021/item/2192-intelligence-community-assessment-on-foreign -threats-to-the-2020-u-s-federal-elections.

"Foreign Actors and Cybercriminals Likely to Spread Disinformation Regarding 2020 Election Results." Federal Bureau of Investigation (FBI) and the Cyber- security and Infrastructure Security Agency (CISA), September 22, 2020. https://www.ic3.gov/Media/Y2020/PSA200922.

Global Engagement Center, U.S. Department of State. *GEC Special Report: Russia's Pillars of Disinformation and Propaganda.* August 2020. https://www .state.gov/russias-pillars-of-disinformation-and-propaganda-report/.

Homeland Threat Assessment. U. S. Department of Homeland Security, October 2020. https://www.dhs.gov/publication/2020-homeland-threat -assessment.

"Joint Statement from the Departments of Justice and Homeland Security Assessing the Impact of Foreign Interference During the 2020 U.S. Elections."

Office of Public Affairs, U. S. Department of Justice, March 16, 2021. https://
www.justice.gov/opa/pr/joint-statement-departments-justice-and-homeland
-security-assessing-impact-foreign.

"NSA and FBI Expose Russian Previously Undisclosed Malware "Drovorub" in
Cybersecurity Advisory." Federal Bureau of Investigation, August 13, 2020.
https://www.fbi.gov/news/press-releases/nsa-and-fbi-expose-russian
-previously-undisclosed-malware-drovorub-in-cybersecurity-advisory.

*Russian Disinformation Attacks on Elections: Lessons from Europe : Hearing Before
the Subcommittee on Europe, Eurasia, Energy, and the Environment of the Committee on Foreign Affairs, House of Representatives, One Hundred Sixteenth Congress, First Session.* July 16, 2019. https://purl.fdlp.gov/GPO
/gp0125541.

"Statement by NCSC Director William Evanina: Election Threat Update for the
American Public." Office of the Director of National Intelligence, August 7,
2020. https://www.dni.gov/index.php/newsroom/press-releases/item/2139
-statement-by-ncsc-director-william-evanina-election-threat-update-for-the
-american-public.

"Treasury Escalates Sanctions Against the Russian Government's Attempts to
Influence U.S. Elections." U. S. Department of the Treasury, April 15, 2021.
https://home.treasury.gov/news/press-releases/jy0126.

"Treasury Sanctions Russia-Linked Election Interference Actors." U.S.
Department of the Treasury, September 10, 2020. https://home.treasury.gov
/news/press-releases/sm1118.

*Worldwide Threats to the Homeland: Hearing Before the Committee on Homeland
Security, House of Representatives, One Hundred Sixteenth Congress, Second
Session.* September 17, 2020. https://purl.fdlp.gov/GPO/gp0154029.

Additional Sources

Bertrand, Natasha. "The Shadowy Operative at the Center of the Russia Scandal."
Atlantic.com, March 29, 2018. https://www.theatlantic.com/politics
/archive/2018/03/the-shadowy-operative-at-the-center-of-the-russia
-scandal/556823/.

Burt, Tom. "New Cyberattacks Targeting U.S. Elections." *On the Issues* (blog),
Microsoft.com, September 10, 2020. https://blogs.microsoft.com/on-the
-issues/2020/09/10/cyberattacks-us-elections-trump-biden/.

Kliman, Daniel, Andrea Kendall-Taylor, Kristine Lee, Joshua Fitt and Carisa
Nietsche. "Dangerous Synergies: Countering Chinese and Russian Digital

Influence Operations." Center for a New American Security, May 7, 2020. https://www.cnas.org/publications/reports/dangerous-synergies.

Lamond, James and Jeremy Venook. "Blunting Foreign Interference Efforts by Learning the Lessons of the Past." Center for American Progress, September 2, 2020. https://www.americanprogress.org/article/blunting-foreign-interference -efforts-learning-lessons-past/.

INDEX

Printed in the USA
CPSIA information can be obtained
at www.ICGtesting.com
LVHW091243041023
758535LV00033B/341